On That Day, Everybody Ate

One Woman's Story
of Hope and Possibility
in Haiti

Margaret Trost

koa books

Koa Books
P.O. Box 822
Kihei, Hawai'i 96753
www.koabooks.com

Publisher's Cataloging-in-Publication Data

Trost, Margaret.
    On that day, everybody ate : one woman's story of hope and
possibility in Haiti / Margaret Trost. -- Kihei, Hawai'i : Koa
Books, c2008.
        p. ; cm.
        ISBN: 978-0-9773338-9-9

        1. Humanitarian assistance, American—Haiti. 2. Food
relief—Haiti. 3. Haiti—Social conditions—1971- 4. Children—
Haiti—Social conditions—1971- 5. What If? Foundation—
History. I. Title.

HV161 .T76 2008
361.9/7294—dc22   0810

1 2 3 4 5 6 7 8 9 / 12 11 10 09 08

Contents

Foreword

This deeply affecting story about an American's coming to terms with her connection to Haiti—and thus to a world of pain and joy and suffering and inspiration— is surprisingly unsentimental, given that her story, and the story of the people she came to know and admire, is at turns wrenching and inspiring.

Traveling from comfortable California to the slums of Port-au-Prince, Margaret Trost encounters, for the first time, an almost biblical poverty, "spread out for miles and miles in all directions." But poverty, she knows, doesn't just happen; poverty has a history, just as people living in poverty have their own stories. Struggling quietly with her own comparative privilege, Trost asks herself, again and again, what forces and events left so many Haitians living on the edge and what, if anything, might make a difference.

On That Day, Everybody Ate is the story of how Margaret Trost answered these questions with the help of her Haitian guides—most of them parishioners of a Catholic church in which the commandment to feed the hungry is taken seriously—and it unfolds like a quiet revelation. As we learn about the family that takes in Trost (and her son and brother), we also learn about her own losses (widowed without warning at 34), her fears (Am I doing enough? How do we live on a fragile planet in which the excesses seen, say, in the Miami airport—all those unfinished meals!—and the hungry slums of Haiti are but an hour and a half apart?), and her growing awareness of how the ostensibly separate worlds of rich and poor, sick and well, hungry and sated, are really one world.

This book should enjoy wide readership as more and more of us who do enjoy comparative privilege become aware of how much so many others struggle simply to survive. This small, polished gem of a book is one compelling answer to many questions about how to inject meaning in our lives without doing damage to history—without ignoring or erasing the ties that bind us all together.

For those already familiar with Haiti, Trost also offers an intimate portrait of this parish of the poor, St. Clare's, and of its leaders, including the courageous and charismatic Father Gerry Jean-Juste, the first Haitian to be ordained a Catholic priest in the United States. Even before the epilogue, which tells of Father Jean-Juste's tribulations after a violent coup and international machinations unseat, yet again, the elected government of Haiti, the reader has been ably guided over the slippery and jagged terrain of modern-day Haiti. Indeed, the country takes its rightful place, alongside Trost's host family, Jean-Juste, and his parishioners, as the source of important lessons for all of us.

But *On That Day, Everybody Ate* is not a history lesson: Trost's account, full of humility even as it is told exclusively in the first person, is above all her own attempts to come to terms with the shock of extreme poverty. It is moving and suffused with optimism and a simple, unvarnished conviction—her own and that of the protagonists she sketches so vividly—that no one should be denied the right to survive and that anyone and everyone can do something to make a difference in the lives of our closest neighbors.

Paul Farmer, MD
Partners In Health
Harvard Medical School
July 2008

PART I

Their lives are going to transform you

Osekou!

On the outskirts of Port-au-Prince, at the top of a hill a mile from the nearest paved road, sits St. Clare's Church. Its pink walls and blue-tinted windows are a welcome site of color and vibrancy in a neighborhood packed with one-room, concrete-block homes. The community, known as Tiplas Kazo, is one in a string of desperately poor sections of Haiti's capital. Dusty, rutted roads wind among the houses. There are few cars and few trees. Smoke fills the air, as residents cook with charcoal in their tiny homes.

On a windy January day, as our van struggles up the steep hillside, slipping on rocks and weaving around potholes, I watch children look up with curiosity from the pebble and marble games they are playing in the dirt. When we round the final corner and park on the side of the road, the exuberant singing of hundreds of women, men, and children streams out of St. Clare's Church as if to greet us.

I had never been to a Catholic Mass before, but after just a couple of days in Port-au-Prince, I was hoping a Haitian service might provide some insight and much-needed sustenance. I'd been one of twelve U.S. citizens volunteering at an orphanage and a hospice, and with one week to go, I was feeling overwhelmed and depressed.

The sanctuary felt like a sauna. I looked for fans and saw them along the butter-yellow walls, but they weren't working. I decided to sit apart from my group and mix in with the congregation, so I squeezed into one of the back rows, my hips pressed against the hips of my neighbors. I'd never seen a church so full. When it was time to stand, we all rose together—glued by our sweat—like one body. We sat down the same way.

I met my pew mates at the beginning of the service, during the welcome and "passing of the peace." I was a little nervous, not sure how I'd be received, but they put me at ease with their smiles, kisses on the cheek, *"Bonjou"*s, and enthusiastic handshakes.

The service went quickly—a lively mixture of singing, praying, a short sermon, and communion. Not understanding a word and not being Catholic, I spent most of the time looking at the parishioners. To my right sat an elderly woman with dark-brown skin and gray-streaked black hair pulled back in a bun. She had a kind face, full of folds and creases, and she was wearing a faded floral dress and a royal blue hat. A few minutes into the Mass, she reached for her purse and pulled out a paper fan, which she waved steadily in my direction. A cinnamon-colored man in his 20s sat to my left. He was tall and very thin, with black pants and a white shirt that hung loosely on him. With a strong, deep voice, he belted out the songs, which he and everyone else knew by heart. A 3-year-old with yellow ribbons in her hair sat in front of me. Although her mother told her not to stare, she couldn't help herself and kept turning around in the pew to give me a shy look. *"Blan,"* she whispered to her mother, which means "white" or "foreigner" in Creole. And that I was—a midwestern 37-year-old mom with dark-blonde hair, blue eyes, and winter-white skin. I did stand out.

During the offering, I watched, amazed, as every man, woman, and child walked up the center aisle to put a coin or two in the wooden box. The congregation was so poor, I wondered how they were able to give so willingly when they lived in homes without plumbing or electricity. In the middle of the procession, a 10-year-old boy just two rows in front of me collapsed. My heart stopped. Had he died? His father calmly picked him up and carried him out the back door, patting his back and whispering in his ear. I never saw them again.

Two hours after the service began, it concluded with a prayer to Saint Jude, the patron saint of desperate situations. When things are at their worst, it is St. Jude you pray to, hoping that together with Jesus, he will make the impossible possible. The smiles on the faces of the children in anticipation of the prayer showed that this was a favorite part of the service. The 3-year-old with yellow ribbons stood up eagerly, along with everyone else, and raised her arms above her head. I did the same.

"St. Jude!" the priest called out in his deep, powerful voice.

"St. Jude!" the congregation responded with equal intensity.

"Pwoblèm nou grav!" (We have a serious problem), the priest said, looking up at the ceiling.

"Pwoblèm nou grav!" 700 men, women, and children responded—their eyes closed and arms outstretched, praying with all their might.

"St. Jude!" the priest called out again.

"St. Jude!" the congregation repeated, their voices rising in unison.

Back and forth, the prayer continued for several minutes, everyone rocking from side to side, eyes shut, concentrating on each word the priest said.

"Pa bliye peyi nou, St. Jude" (Don't forget our country, St. Jude). The priest's white robe fluttered, as a breeze came through the sanctuary.

"Pa bliye peyi nou, St. Jude." The congregation's voices filled every corner of the church, resonating off the walls, through the open windows, and out into the neighborhood. People a mile away could hear our prayer.

"Pa bliye pèp Ayisien, St. Jude" (Don't forget the Haitian people, St. Jude).

"Pa bliye pèp Ayisien, St. Jude." Everyone swayed, their arms waving above their heads, each phrase building on the previous one, the call and response reaching a crescendo.

The priest spun around and faced the glass painting of St. Jude that was placed up high, just to the right of the cross in the front of the sanctuary. He let out a thunderous plea.

"St. Jude, osekou!"

"St. Jude, osekou!" the congregation cried back, holding the *"koooooooooouuuuuuu"* for several seconds.

"Amen. Alelouya! Amen Alelouya!"

"Amen. Alelouya! Amen Alelouya!"

Then everyone clapped loudly. Exhausted and inspired, I clapped with them, tears filling my eyes.

After the benediction, as I prepared to leave, I turned to the elderly woman who had greeted me in broken English at the beginning of the service, and asked her the meaning of the prayer's final word, *osekou*. The passion with which it was said made me wonder. She looked into my eyes, lifted her finger, and drew three letters in the air: S . . . O . . . S.

Seeds and Signs

I've often wondered how far back the seeds of Haiti were planted inside me. The children of the Tiplas Kazo community in Port-au-Prince have become such an important part of my life that I like to think that over the years I had been preparing for my connection with them.

Some of the seeds surely were sown when I was a child, sitting week after week in the second pew on the left side, right in front of the pulpit, at St. Paul's United Church of Christ in Chicago. My father was the minister, and I spent my first eighteen years listening to his sermons. Dad always emphasized putting faith into action by reaching out to those in need and working for social justice.

Perhaps more seeds were planted during childhood trips to the Cayman Islands, where my grandparents had a small cottage on the beach. The heat, the sugarcane, the palm trees, the humidity, the blue-green waters of the Caribbean—I loved them all. I spent hours on the dock watching tiny iridescent fish swim near the water's surface. At night, I sat on the shore staring at the stars, listening to the waves, feeling the tropical wind, imagining myself as a Caymanian so I'd never have to leave.

I studied French in high school. I hadn't spoken a word of it for twenty years, but all those verb conjugations started to come back as soon as I stepped off the plane in Port-au-Prince.

I was invited to go to Haiti in the spring of 1999, and my response took less than a second. It was one of those times when my heart spoke before my mind had time to catch up. I was helping out at a retreat and ran into a friend of my father's, Bryan Sirchio, a minister and musician. I hadn't seen him in years, but I instantly remembered a song he'd sung years earlier, called *Staring at My Overflowing Plate.* It described a scene at a Haitian restaurant—an American visitor was served a large plate of food, and just as he was about to eat, he looked out the window and saw hungry children with their noses pressed against the windowpane, staring at his meal. The waiter came over quickly and pulled down the shade, so they wouldn't be seen. Bryan's song was about how we pull the shade down and pretend not to see the suffering of the world.

> *It's so easy not to see you*
> *Close you out like a shade in the window*
> *Your condition seems so foreign*
> *Are you lazy? Why are you poor?*
> *Someone said you and I are connected*

That your hunger is linked to my fatness
But how can that be—I never met you
I don't know your name
I've got problems of my own
I'm so busy—I do good things
And I don't know if I can make room
In my life for your misery
Someone said that the whole world is changing
For you no longer will stand to be used
But talk like that—it makes me frightened
Scared what I might lose

I'd never thought about Haiti before this song and hadn't thought about it much after, but the moment I saw Bryan, the hungry children looking through the restaurant window came back to me. I asked him whether he still sang the song and if he'd been to Haiti recently. He told me that he still went several times a year, and sometimes brought people with him. Then he invited me to go with him on his next trip. He said it almost in passing, but my heart spoke and I said yes.

Bryan explained that it would be a two-week "pilgrimage of reverse mission" to Port-au-Prince. It was called "reverse" because it was designed to be transformational for the participants. It would involve volunteering at an orphanage or with sick adults during the day and learning more about Haiti through various speakers at night. There would be plenty of time for reflection and journal writing. Witnessing life in Haiti, Bryan said, would probably raise all sorts of questions and feelings about life, faith, wealth, and poverty. "Their lives are going to transform you." That's exactly what I wanted.

On the surface, I appeared successful as a businesswoman and parent. But beneath, I was struggling, going through the motions of life with a broken heart that I thought would never heal. At the time of Bryan's invitation, I needed help and was searching for something—I didn't know exactly what—but something that would move me forward out of the rut I'd been in. This trip could help. It was certainly worth a try.

Eighteen months earlier, my husband had died. It was unexpected and devastating. He was 36. I was 34. Our son had just turned 5. On a warm September evening, as we watched the sun set in the countryside and talked about our commitment to slow down so we could enjoy each other more, I had no idea that five minutes later, Rich would be gone. The coroner never identified what triggered his asthma attack. Whatever the allergen was, it was so toxic, it killed him in less than five minutes.

Never would I have imagined that I'd be a widow in my mid-30s, overwhelmed with grief. I'd always thought Rich and I would age gracefully into our 80s or 90s, spending our lives together enjoying fulfilling careers, volunteering for meaningful causes, raising two or three children, and then retiring to a beach house like the one my grandparents had. That vision vanished as I struggled desperately to blow air into his lungs. Suddenly, my future disappeared. I had no energy to think about anything except taking care of our son, Luke, and doing the minimum to keep my home-based health and wellness business going so I could pay the bills.

I stumbled through those first few weeks and months, numb and without direction. Searching for meaning in Rich's death, I pored over countless spiritual books, hoping they might shed light on why. I wanted to believe that Rich's death had some purpose that would inspire me to move forward, make plans, and create a new future for Luke and me. Every day, I searched for "signs" that God and Rich were with me, talking to me, and that, at some level, all was well. Before long, everything became a sign—a butterfly, a cloud formation, a ray of light in the corner of my bedroom, a thought that didn't sound like one of mine, a bird lingering at my window, an unusual dream. But even though I did feel reassured of God's loving presence, I suffered at a level I'd never known before.

I felt stuck, and prayed for more signs—hoping they would help me see my way out of my grief. When the invitation to go on the "reverse mission" came, I jumped at the chance. It seemed like this could be my sign. Going to Haiti was so "out of the blue," it felt oddly right. I didn't know where it would lead, but the experience would take me far away from Cottage Grove, Wisconsin, where I lived, to a place completely unknown. It sounded perfect. Maybe attending to the suffering of others might shift some attention away from my own pain. I filled out the application and sent in the deposit.

In the nine months that passed between my saying yes to the "reverse mission" and actually getting on the plane, I didn't think much about the trip. Shortly after I saw Bryan, I moved to the San Francisco Bay Area to live with my sister. I was overwhelmed with the move, enrolling Luke in first grade, running my business, and beginning a new life in California. Every minute of every day was packed with work and parenting responsibilities. I seemed to be racing everywhere, often late, out of breath, exhausted, and stressed. As the trip to Haiti approached, I wondered what I had been thinking when I said yes, and I thought about canceling. But I didn't.

When the morning came to fly to Port-au-Prince, I grabbed all the material I should have read in advance, packed a small suitcase of hot-weather clothes, waved good-bye to Luke and my mom, who had flown out to take care of him, and headed off in a whirlwind for the airport.

In-flight History Lesson

As I flew from San Francisco to Miami, I thought about how little I knew about Haiti. I'd seen news reports years before of "boat people" struggling to get to Florida, but I couldn't even remember what had caused their exodus. I knew that Haiti shared an island with the Dominican Republic, and that it was tiny, about the size of Maryland, but that was about it.

I began to read statistics: Three-quarters of Haitians live on less than $2 per day. Four and a half million people—over half the population (56 percent)—live on less than $1 per day. Safe drinking water is not regularly accessible to over a third of the population. The countryside is 97 percent deforested. Haiti has a 70 percent unemployment rate, a 50 percent illiteracy rate, and the worst health statistics in the Western world. About 75 percent of Haiti's farmable land is owned by just 5 percent of its inhabitants. Nearly half of Haiti's wealth is controlled by 1 percent of the population.

Then, I pulled out a stack of background material and a book Bryan had sent months before—*The Uses of Haiti*, written by physician and anthropologist Dr. Paul Farmer. Dr. Farmer is a professor at Harvard Medical School who since 1983 has lived and worked in Haiti, where he became a founding director of Partners In Health, a renowned nonprofit that works with Haitians to build clinics and provide free health care services for the poor in Haiti and elsewhere.

Dr. Farmer's text was mind-opening and heartbreaking. It detailed the complex history that helped explain why Haiti is the most underdeveloped country in the Western Hemisphere. It critiqued U.S. foreign policy and showed how U.S. companies and Haiti's wealthy elite profited continually at the expense of the poor. By the end of the book, I understood his title—*The Uses of Haiti*—because Haiti has been used and exploited by others throughout its history.

Haitians are the descendants of African slaves. In the 18th century, Haiti—called Saint-Domingue then—was the wealthiest French colony in the world, providing two-thirds of Europe's tropical produce. In 1791, the slaves, led by Toussaint Louverture, organized and launched what became the first and only successful slave revolution in the world. The war against their French colonizers lasted thirteen years. Over 200,000 people were killed. The country's infrastructure was destroyed and agricultural productivity stopped.

When the war ended, in 1804, Haiti became the world's first black republic and Latin America's first sovereign nation. It also became the first nation to ban slavery and to declare itself a haven for runaway slaves and other oppressed people. I couldn't believe I'd never read about this in school.

But the world's powers did not support Haiti. For the next sixty years, the U.S. refused to recognize Haiti as an independent republic, because the U.S. had slaves of its own and was afraid they might be inspired by Haiti's example. A diplomatic quarantine, threatening visits from German, French, British, and American gunboats, and a growing economic dependency on the U.S. and Europe made it impossible to rebuild the country.

I was astonished to read that France demanded that Haiti pay 150 million gold francs to compensate for French losses during the war. If Haiti didn't comply, France would not recognize Haiti's independence, and it threatened to return and reinstitute slavery. The sum of 150 million francs was ten times Haiti's annual budget. Desperate for trading partners, and with the possibility of another French invasion and the restoration of slavery, Haiti's leaders borrowed from French bankers (as required by the agreement) to begin repaying the "debt." By the end of the 19th century, 80 percent of Haiti's national revenue was allocated to repaying debts. It took Haiti 125 years to pay off the debt to France (estimated at a value of $21 billion today with interest and inflation calculated in), and the effects on the society were devastating.

The Haitian Revolution was followed by nearly two centuries of power struggle among various elite factions and the masses of the poor, who never gave up their dream of full participation. On the heels of a popular uprising, the U.S. Marines invaded and occupied Haiti from 1915 to 1934. A new Haitian army, created and trained by the U.S. during the occupation, became the dominant power after the Marines left. There ensued a series of U.S.-backed dictatorships, including the brutal Duvalier regimes that lasted from 1957 to 1986. When I read about "Papa Doc" Duvalier and his son "Baby Doc," who succeeded him, their names sounded vaguely familiar. They had received millions in aid from the U.S., the World Bank, and the International Monetary Fund over the years, but had used little of it to benefit the poor majority. Instead, it supported fraud, corruption, and the oppression of any opposition. Their feared militia, called the Tonton Macoutes, was known for killing all opponents. Thousands of Haitians fled the country for their lives.

In the mid-1980s, Haitians began to organize in opposition to the dictatorship. Through tremendous courage and tenacity, their marches and strikes led to the overthrow of "Baby Doc" Duvalier. Meanwhile, a soft-spoken Catholic priest was beginning to touch hearts and raise consciousness, leading to the mobilization of the poor throughout the country. When I began reading about the rise of Jean-Bertrand Aristide, it seemed that finally something positive was about to happen.

Aristide advocated for the millions of impoverished Haitians. He challenged the status quo, pointing out that Haiti's poverty was a result of its history and the tiny ruling class that had always controlled social and economic power. In Haiti's first democratic election, in 1990, Aristide was elected president with 67 percent of the vote. For the first time, the poor majority played a role in shaping national policy. Aristide's government quickly initiated adult literacy and public health programs, and set out to raise the minimum wage, create land reform, and end corruption. These initiatives did not make him popular among wealthy business owners (in Haiti and abroad), landowners, or the Haitian military.

Just seven months after the democratic government was inaugurated, a violent coup led by members of the Haitian military forced Aristide into exile. The coup was followed by three years of repression and violence by the Haitian military and by paramilitary groups. It was later revealed that one of the top paramilitary leaders, Emmanuel Constant, was working with the CIA. Tens of thousands of Haitians tried to escape during this time. These were the "boat people" I'd seen on TV.

Escalating repression, a flood of unwelcome refugees in Florida, no signs of the brutal de facto military government ending its reign of terror, and the growing international solidarity for the Haitian democratic process led the U.S., with support from the UN and international community, to return President Aristide to power. This reinstatement came with conditions, including accepting economic "structural adjustment" programs, some of which would privatize Haiti's publicly owned utilities and would slash tariffs.

In September 1994, 20,000 U.S. troops entered Haiti, and a month later President Aristide returned to serve out the remainder of his presidency. Back in office, he dismantled the much-hated Haitian army and focused on improving the lives of the poor majority. His term ended shortly thereafter, in

February 1996. Power was transferred peacefully for the first time in Haiti's infant democracy to René Préval, who was just finishing his five-year term as president when I visited the first time. Another presidential election was just a few months away. Aristide was running again and was expected to win.

I put the book down in a daze and stared at the clouds. How could I live in the U.S. and know so little about our neighbor only 600 miles away—an hour-and-a-half flight from Miami?

Fear crept into my mind. I had lots of questions for Bryan, the first being: Was Haiti safe? Haiti had such a violent history and the U.S. government had contributed to the suffering in so many ways throughout the last 200 years. Did Haitians resent Americans? How would it feel to be an overfed white American among people who struggle daily for food and clean water? I'd just spent the daily income of about twenty Haitians on magazines and snacks at the airport in San Francisco. I had more on my airline lunch tray than most Haitians ate in a day. I felt nervous and guilty, and we hadn't even landed. As the plane sped along in air-conditioned, high-tech comfort, I wondered if there had ever been a day—just one day—in my life when I had experienced real hunger.

M'Grangou

As the plane descended into Port-au-Prince's Toussaint Louverture International Airport, I watched the sparkly blue Caribbean turn to a murky brown just off the coast. From overhead, I could easily see that the mountains were stripped of trees. With most of Haiti's trees cut down, there was no root system to soak up water, and when it rained, the precious topsoil washed into the ocean. This was one reason why Haitian peasants struggled to feed their families. Their soil was gone.

Toussaint Louverture Airport's tiny baggage claim area was chaotic and hot. I found my luggage quickly and followed our group out of the building. As I walked out onto the street, a crowd of men of all ages approached, pleading to carry my bag. Before I could respond, four of them reached for my small suitcase and disappeared into the crowd. I ran after them, weaving through dozens of people, worried I might never see my suitcase again, but at the end of the walkway I spotted them next to our group's van. Bryan was giving them a tip. *"Mèsi, mèsi"* (Thank you), they said with both desperation and gratitude in their eyes.

I felt sick to my stomach, and my heart was pounding. When I looked at my hands, they were shaking. I was afraid, overwhelmed by the mass of people that surrounded me, the smell of burning garbage, the heat. Sweat dripping down my forehead, I squeezed into a seat in the back of the van, clutched my backpack against my chest, and wondered if I'd made a mistake coming here. When the van finally pulled away from the curb, I was relieved to be moving again.

The slow, bumpy ride to the hotel gave me time to center myself. I closed my eyes and breathed deeply, trying to slow down my heart and remember why I'd come to Haiti. Helping out at the hospice had been my motivation. Reverse mission. Willing a positive attitude, I relaxed my shoulders, sat up in my seat, and started to take in the streets of Haiti's capital.

The roads were treacherous. Gigantic potholes, open sewers, boulders, no traffic lights or sidewalks—I'd never seen anything like it. Hundreds of people lined the streets. Groups of men studied the engines of stalled cars or repaired ripped tires. A chairmaker and a man creating bed frames out of iron worked next to each other. Women and young girls in dresses and head wraps carried water jugs on their heads, maneuvering gracefully around people and rubble in the street. Vendors, packed along the side of the road, sold mangoes and sugarcane, fabric and charcoal, waiting patiently for the occasional customer.

Brightly painted minibuses and pickup trucks, called "tap-taps," inched along, stuffed with travelers. Each time a tap-tap stopped, I watched in amazement as more people piled in. How they fit, I do not know. I was struck by the phrases, some written in English, that decorated the buses: "Thank you Jesus," "Pray," "One love," "Be cheerful," "Patience."

We drove past shacks and decaying buildings, dodged around ragged chunks of concrete in the road and piles of garbage 6 feet high baking in the sun. I started breathing through my mouth. Heaps of gravel and half-dug trenches showed signs of development here and there, but, overall, the city's infrastructure was ancient and broken.

Each time our van slowed down, barefoot children wearing torn T-shirts ran up to our windows and peeked in. With palms outstretched, they cried out, *"M'grangou,"* which means "I'm hungry" in Creole. We were told not to give them any money, that if we did, our van would be swarmed with kids and it wouldn't be safe for them in the street. Bryan assured us we'd have other opportunities to share our resources with nonprofits that provided services to children. The out-stretched palms by our window remained empty. I couldn't look in the children's pleading eyes for more than a second and was relieved when our van started moving again. These children were Luke's age. I learned later that they represented a handful of the thousands of orphans who roam the streets of Port-au-Prince.

At dinner that night, I didn't eat or talk much. None of us did. Every muscle in my body was tense. My mind raced, trying to sort through what I'd seen. I'd been to Nicaragua and Mexico but had never seen anything like this. Poverty wasn't isolated to one section of town. It was everywhere—spread out for miles and miles in all directions. The contrast from Miami to Port-au-Prince was beyond words. My heart hurt. I felt like sobbing, but couldn't shed a tear. I was in shock. Reading about massive poverty was one thing. Witnessing people struggling to survive was quite another.

Before we got up from the table, Bryan asked us to scrape all the food we didn't eat onto an empty plate. I asked if I should include food that I'd picked at with my fork. Bryan nodded. Our waiter bowed his head in thanks as he quickly cleared the table and took the overflowing plates away. He would bring our leftovers to his children.

Son Fils

The next morning, we drove to volunteer at Son Fils, Port-au-Prince's Home for the Destitute and the Dying. The hospice's small courtyard was full of frail men, some shaving, others playing dominoes. The Missionaries of Charity, the order founded by Mother Teresa, ran this two-story facility. Patients came from all over Port-au-Prince in hope that there might be a bed for them. Care was free. With limited medication—just whatever was donated—the nuns provided a loving environment for people to heal or die.

I went up to the second-floor women's area with three other volunteers from our group. As we rounded the corner, a nun carrying a tray of cooked rice greeted us. She looked just like Mother Teresa in her light-blue-and-white sari and habit. "Welcome. We're glad you're here. You can help change the sheets in the rooms. We have extra nail polish and lotion if you'd like to paint the ladies' nails or give massages when you're finished." She smiled and walked away. I couldn't take my eyes off her. Her glow brought tears to my eyes and helped calm my nerves. How was it that, surrounded by all this suffering, she could be so bright and peaceful? My jaw relaxed a bit and my shoulders settled. She'd helped melt some of the fear and shock I was carrying.

The infirmary was simple. It looked like overnight camp, with beds lined up neatly next to each other. A volunteer from a Canadian group was singing Creole songs with three of the patients. She told us that this room housed women who were sick, but not about to die. They were in the next room. She also told us that many of the women suffered from tuberculosis. A shortage of safe drinking water, inadequate sanitation, and severe malnutrition left Haitians vulnerable to TB and many other diseases. Some patients also had HIV/AIDS, one of the main causes of adult deaths in Haiti. It is believed that AIDS arrived in Haiti through infected tourists. The combination of HIV and tuberculosis is particularly deadly. With proper medicine, recovery from TB is almost assured. But most Haitians couldn't afford treatment, so they died.

I lifted a mattress to tuck in the sheet and discovered one patient's small collection of personal items hidden beneath— a pair of carefully folded underwear, a rosary, a comb, and a hair clip. That was it. Was this all she had with her, or all she owned? Glancing at the patients sitting on the balcony, I wondered who slept in the bed I was making. They were all wearing the same light-blue dresses—a gift from a U.S. donor. Most were in their 20s or 30s. Some were so thin it looked as though the slightest breeze could carry them away. Others seemed okay, until they coughed the deep, barking, painful cough of tuberculosis.

Not feeling ready to venture next door, I stayed put and began giving manicures to two young women who looked like good friends. They came up to me and showed me their chipped, royal blue fingernail polish. *"Mal. Mal"* (Bad), they said. I nodded and smiled. They pointed eagerly to the bright red polish I was holding.

Since they had enough energy to sit up, I handed them several cotton balls and a bottle of nail polish remover. The woman on my right carefully divided one of the cotton balls into four sections, as if it was a precious gift. With just one of these sections, she removed the polish from all ten of her nails. She handed the bottle and another quarter of the cotton ball to her friend. Then she handed me the other two sections and the other cotton balls I had originally given her. She didn't need them. It had never occurred to me that you could remove nail polish with just a quarter of a cotton ball. I usually go through at least one, if not two, per hand.

A lump lodged in my throat and I felt tears rush to my eyes. I took a quick breath and held it, hoping my eyes wouldn't overflow. I didn't want them to think something was wrong. They were enjoying themselves and so was I— three women sharing a manicure. But something was wrong. I thought about how different our lives were and wondered how many times a day I consume three or four times more than is really necessary. I'd never appreciated the value of a cotton ball before. My drawers were stuffed with them. I think I had as many bottles of vitamins and aspirin and Band-Aids in my cupboard as these nuns had in their whole facility. I took another deep breath and forced myself to apply the polish onto these beautiful young ladies' nails.

"Bèl. Bèl. Mèsi," they said when I finished. I smiled, but avoided eye contact, afraid I'd start crying. When I left the room I watched them over my shoulder, holding their hands up and admiring their new bright-red nails.

Beautiful Mother

On my next visit to Son Fils, I went into the intensive care room. I was nervous and kept reminding myself that I could handle sitting next to people who were about to die. After all, I'd knelt next to Rich in his final moments. I should be able to do this too.

The room was quiet. All I could hear was my sandals clicking on the cement floor. Most of the women were asleep, their bodies so thin that I could barely make them out under the sheets. I looked for medical equipment—ventilators, IVs, heart monitors—but didn't see any. I decided to go to a bed on the far side of the room near a window.

As I sat down, a young woman opened her eyes to greet me. Her lids were heavy and they closed again quickly. I took her hand—skin and bones—and studied her stunning face. I wondered how old she was and what disease had brought her here. She looked like a model with her almond-shaped eyes and high cheekbones. Her eyes opened again. I held up massage cream, and she blinked yes. My hands shook as I gently massaged her hand and then her arm, afraid I might hurt her if I pressed too hard. When I got to her upper arm, I noticed it wasn't any bigger than her wrist. I circled my hand around it, right near the armpit, to see if my thumb and index finger were able to touch. They did. Easily.

She motioned to her sternum, asking me to massage there, too. I hesitated, thinking that it seemed too intimate for strangers, but she reached out for my hand and pulled it toward her chest. As I moved her nightgown over to the side, I saw the familiar stretch marks of a mother. *"Enfants?"* I asked. *"Oui,"* she whispered. *"Trois."* Three children. I wonder who's taking care of them? How she must miss them. I wished I could remember more of my French so I could ask more questions. She asked if I had children. *"Oui. Un."* She smiled and closed her eyes. I guessed she was thinking of her children, wondering what they were doing and how they were. I pressed gently on her sternum, afraid I'd break it, but she held her hand over mine, encouraging me to push harder. Then she let out one of those wrenching coughs. She had TB. The pressing on her sternum must have provided some relief. A few minutes later, she fell asleep.

Being with her reminded me of a day shortly after Rich died when a friend stopped by with a bottle of hand lotion. It had been a particularly difficult day emotionally and I didn't feel like talking. She understood, put her arm around me, led me to a chair, and gently, in silence, massaged my hands. When she finished, she gave me a long hug and left. No words were needed. I never forgot her kindness and felt, in a small way, I was passing it on to this young woman.

The moans of another woman two beds down brought me back to present time. As I started to walk toward her, I passed a patient wrapped tightly in a sheet, like a mummy. I stopped and stared. I couldn't see her face and didn't detect any breathing. Had she died? My heart started to pound and a wave of heat went through my body. The already stifling temperature felt as if it went up 10 more degrees. The reality of impending death throughout the room suddenly hit me. I didn't know what to do. I looked around to see if there were any nuns nearby, but I was alone.

Not sure where to go, I decided to keep walking to the bed of the moaning woman. I approached her slowly and timidly knelt down next to her. Would I know what to do if she reached out to me or if she pushed me away? I turned to look at the mother of three, and considered going back to her cot. It was easier to sit with someone silent and sleeping than to be next to someone so clearly in pain. I forced myself to stay put.

Back and forth the moaning woman rocked in the fetal position. Weren't there any painkillers? She looked over at me, and I motioned to the lotion, but she shook her head no. I put my hand gently on her arm. I didn't know what else to do. Tears dripped down her cheeks. Her eyes were blood-shot, revealing her physical agony and her despair. I tried to think of words in French that would convey how sorry I was that she was hurting, but I couldn't remember any, so I sat there silently. Suddenly, she lifted her head, looked me in the eye, and spoke in English. "I have nothing," she said, enun-ciating every word. "No shoes... No dress... No money..." She lay back down on the pillow and stared at the ceiling. "I have big problems." Her words startled me. I hadn't expected English, and I didn't know what to say. I just held her hand and waited for more. "I want to brush my—" she whispered as she pointed to her teeth and then her hair. I nodded. She started to say something else, but a coughing fit overtook her. Then she rolled over, exhausted, and closed her eyes.

I quickly left the room. As I stood on the balcony, my body shook with frustration and anger. Frustration because there was nothing I could do to help these women. Anger that this level of suffering existed—not only at Son Fils, but throughout Haiti. These women were dying young and alone—without their husbands or their children, without painkillers, IVs, doctors, or nurses. They couldn't afford to go to a hospital, and even if they could, there was only one doctor for every 10,000 Haitians, a statistic I couldn't get my mind around, it was so outrageous. In the U.S., the ratio is 1 to 350.

I leaned against the balcony railing, holding my head in my hands. Part of me wanted to run and get on the next plane. Another part of me couldn't leave the women at Son Fils.

Searching for something positive, I told myself that at least they had a loving environment to die in. Or maybe they'd get better. What if a shipment of donated medicine arrived tomorrow and saved their lives? What if that mother with the beautiful eyes made a miraculous recovery and went home to her three children? What if the woman I was just with regained her strength so she could brush her teeth and hair? But that day, I couldn't bring my heart to believe in possibilities.

Later, when we returned to the hotel, I was grateful to be separated from the rest of the city. I sat in a beach chair by the pool and stared at the palm trees waving overhead. I couldn't motivate myself to write in my journal. Others in our group felt the same. We were all lost in our own thoughts—serious and silent.

Cité Soleil

Not far from the government buildings of downtown Port-au-Prince, near the sea, is a massive shantytown called Cité Soleil, built on a landfill that stretches as far as the eye can see. As many as 300,000 people live there. Bryan was involved in a community development project and had connections that made it possible for our group to visit.

Our stay was only three hours, but that was long enough to witness the devastation. Before meeting at a community center to talk with residents, we walked fifteen minutes through the dense maze of shacks on our way to a tiny artisan shop. Our guides, residents of Cité Soleil, told us to stick close together and to stay in a single-file line. Poverty here is the worst it gets in Haiti and tensions ran high. It was not a safe place to be alone. One guide walked at the front of the line; the other stayed at the back.

From what I could see, most of the shelters were made of cardboard, tar paper, and pieces of tin or plastic, patched together to form tiny, one-room shacks. Some homes had cinder blocks for walls, but they looked like they'd crumble if you leaned on them. There weren't many windows, so it was hard to see inside, but occasionally I caught a glimpse of a chair or a table or a pot. The floors were dirt, and a piece of ripped cloth often served as a door. No one seemed to have electricity, running water, or toilets. The smell of human waste was thick and nauseating.

Someone said that Mother Teresa called this 2.5-square-mile area "the poorest spot on earth." I believed it. There were no sidewalks or even roads leading to the artisan shop. We followed a narrow path that ran between the houses, which were less than a foot apart from each other. I tried not to stare at the people we walked by, but it was hard not to. The scene was bleak beyond anything I'd ever imagined.

Later we were told that as many as a dozen people might live in one shack. At night, they had to rotate sleeping on the floor because there wasn't space for everyone to lie down at once. During the rainy season, when the riverbed and the raw sewage ditches that run between the shacks overflow and the roofs leak, these homes flood, and the dirt floors turn into sewage-drenched mud.

We wove our way through the maze of shacks, passing frail mothers holding babies and young children playing in the dirt without toys. Some of the children had bloated bellies and a reddish tint to their hair—signs of malnutrition and starvation. My eyes met some of the residents and we exchanged nods and sometimes a *"Bonjou."* Their voices were quiet and resigned, their eyes full of despair.

I was walking briskly along with the group, in a daze, when a naked 5-year-old girl with pigtails approached from the side and stopped in front of me. She was carrying a yellow plastic bowl of urine, and she needed to lean over the path I was on to pour it into the ditch that ran in front of her shack. She looked up at me with big brown eyes. I mouthed

"Bonjou," and she nodded, but didn't smile. Carefully she poured the contents of her bowl. The urine splashed onto her bare feet and onto my sneakers. Then she turned and walked back a few feet, disappearing behind her cloth door.

I felt light-headed, queasy from the stench all around me, and I could hardly breathe. Scared, overwhelmed, and outraged by what I was seeing, I didn't know what to do but keep walking. How could conditions like this be allowed to exist? If the world knew, surely it would do something!

I learned later that many of the residents in Cité Soleil were peasants. Unable to grow crops in the eroded countryside, they came to Port-au-Prince in search of work, food, and a better life for their children. But they were met with an even worse situation. I had no idea how they survived. The cramped spaces. The hunger. The filthy ditches. The flies. The disease. The heat. I couldn't even begin to imagine what it would be like to give birth or raise children here.

Finally, we arrived at the art store, a one-room concrete-block structure without windows. I walked into the tiny space, and, once my eyes adjusted to the darkness, I was able to see paintings and woodcarvings on display. The artwork, all created by residents of Cité Soleil, was, to my surprise, colorful and bright, beautiful and full of life. Paintings of the countryside, the sea, palm trees, and exotic flowers leaned against the wall. Woodcarvings of women cradling children or carrying food in baskets on their heads were neatly placed side by side on a table. Metal cutouts of brightly painted fish and parrots were so vibrant they looked alive.

In the corner I spotted a small painting of a Haitian neighborhood. A husband dressed in striped pants and a blue shirt stood next to his wife, who wore a pretty blouse and skirt with a matching ribbon in her hair. They were outside their little white house. As I moved closer to the painting, I could see that the house had strong walls and a solid roof, windows, and a wood door. It was surrounded by beautiful flowers and a healthy tree. In the distance were other sturdy houses with small yards around them. Birds flew overhead and a mountain range was in the distance. Even the oppressiveness of Cité Soleil had not snuffed out this artist's vision of hope.

I bought the painting and several other pieces, wanting to support the artists of Cité Soleil and their vision of beauty and life in the midst of overwhelming misery. I hoped the sale of the painting would help feed their children and make life a little more bearable—at least for a while. But I also felt uncomfortable reaching into my pocket for money—the American consumer, standing in the middle of the poorest spot on earth.

That night, I dreamed I was in a hospital, lying on a gurney. I pulled myself up onto my elbows and saw that my chest was cut open. I could see my heart—damaged, bleeding, and barely beating. I tried to scream to get the attention of the doctors, but no sound came out. No one heard me. No one saw me. I was forgotten in the corner. As I tried to sit up to grab the sleeve of a doctor who was walking by, hoping to get his attention to help me, I woke up. Images of the little girl with the yellow plastic bowl and the children on the street pleading *"M'grangou"* flooded my mind. I spent the rest of the night staring above my bed at the broken ceiling fan.

Holding Hands

Morning finally arrived. My head throbbed from lack of sleep, and my heart ached, reminding me of my dream. I considered spending the day in my hotel room, but when I thought of the mother of three lying on her cot near the window, I threw my sheet off, got up, and got in the van for the ride to Son Fils.

As I walked to the intensive care room, I tiptoed carefully around a group of women who were healthy enough to sit in the fresh air on the narrow balcony. The two friends I'd met a few days before were taking turns braiding each other's hair. They nodded with recognition and proudly showed me their nails, still bright red and unchipped.

I went straight to the back of the room where the mother of three slept. With all the motionless bodies lying under white sheets, the room reminded me of a morgue. A volunteer offered me plastic gloves, but I shook my head, hating the idea of one more layer between my friend and me.

She looked frailer than before. Her eyelids lifted a fraction and then fell shut. I reached for her hand and slipped it in mine. Slowly her lips curled in a smile. I don't know how long I sat next to her, watching the sheet rise and fall with each shallow breath she took. As the minutes passed, my breathing fell in sync with hers and everything quieted down. My mind became still. My body didn't flinch. I felt no desire to move or talk. I felt calm and—was I happy? How could I be, with all the sickness and impending death around me and the memories of Cité Soleil still fresh in my mind? But I think I was. I felt filled up. It seemed impossible, but for that moment, I felt completely at peace. Time stopped and nothing mattered more than sitting on the cot holding her hand.

It must have been an hour later that a visit from a guest doctor brought me out of my stillness. He was gentle and kind, speaking quietly in Creole to each patient as he went from bed to bed with his stethoscope. I detected a Canadian accent as I overheard him give instructions in English to a nun, who was taking notes on a clipboard. I wondered what it must feel like to be a doctor with no medicine to give patients. The TB and HIV drugs that were needed to save these women were not on the shelf. I hoped painkillers had arrived overnight so he could prescribe something to make their days less miserable.

He lingered over a young woman who was lying in a cot near me. She looked about 18 years old and was frightened as he examined her. Rail thin, her body was barely notice-able under the sheet, except for a tiny bulge at her belly. I thought it might be a tumor. The doctor pulled a small de-vice out of his bag and placed it on her stomach. A few sec-onds later, a sound filled the room. I'd recognize it anywhere. *Thump-thump thump-thump thump-thump.* He looked amazed. So was I. A baby!

Remembering the exhilaration of hearing Luke's heart beat for the first time during one of my prenatal appoint-ments, I wondered what was going through this mother's mind. I didn't know whether to smile or cry. Her baby's heart sounded strong. But she was dying. The doctor's face was full of concern as he whispered something to the nun and left the room. I turned back to my friend and squeezed her hand, hoping to return to that sense of peace I'd felt so strongly just a few minutes earlier.

But I couldn't do it. My emotions swung from one ex-treme to another. Joy at the thought of a baby. Grief at the reality that the baby and mother would probably die. Hope that maybe the doctor could help. Despair at knowing he had no equipment or medicine to work with. My mind searched for ways I might help, but I was overwhelmed by the com-plexity of the problems. In a few days, I'd be leaving and would never see these women again. I was returning to my son and our comfortable life with cabinets filled with food and a doctor only a phone call away.

The mother of three must have felt the growing tension in my neck and shoulders as these thoughts filled my mind, because she opened her eyes and smiled at me. Her warm, loving expression seemed to be asking me to stop thinking and just hold her hand. I pushed all the other thoughts away and tried to settle back into the moment with her. Two mothers from completely different lives together on a cot, connected. I felt the muscles in my body relax again, including my heart. Love flowed between us. I could feel it and knew that I wasn't just reaching out to her, offering my hand. She was also reaching out to me, offering hers.

Butterfly

Morning prayers at Son Fils began at 10:30. Those who were strong enough lifted themselves to a sitting position so they could see the two nuns standing near the doorway. A wooden cross and a picture of Mother Teresa hung on the wall behind them. Most of the women remained on their backs with rosaries wrapped around their wrists. I watched my friend to see if she would wake up, but she didn't move.

The prayer began with just the two nuns, but soon many voices joined in the rhythmic flow of words that I didn't understand but found comforting. They came from every corner of the room. The prayer transitioned into a song the women knew well and sang enthusiastically. I was amazed by the strength they found to sing.

Suddenly, a deep, almost haunting voice joined in, much louder than all the others. It was from the woman in the cot next to me, the one I thought might be dead a few days earlier, whose body was wrapped from head to toe in a sheet cocoon. I'd glanced over at her throughout the morning as I held my friend's hand. I'd watched the outline of her body in the sheet, trying to discern breathing. Nothing. She had been deadly quiet. But her voice was now the strongest in the infirmary. She belted out each Creole word with a force and intensity that made the small room feel like a cathedral.

When the song ended, the nuns slipped out, and the room quickly quieted. I could hear the soft, shallow breathing of my friend, her hand in mine. One by one, each patient closed her eyes. Only one woman was unable to rest—the deep-voiced woman lying an arm's length away.

Her back faced me, but I could see she was in significant pain. I wondered if I should reach out as I watched her fidget and wince, struggling to get comfortable. Slowly she rolled in my direction. Her chestnut eyes, wet with tears, stared at me through a small slit in the sheet. She pulled the sheet tight around her shoulders and face, revealing the skin on her swollen hands. It was raw—light pink, infected. It looked like it was peeling off—even on her fingertips. A fly circled the opening around her eyes, and she moaned as she tried to shoo it away. I leaned over and waved my hand, relieved to be able to do something more than stare.

I wanted to go to another part of the room where her pain couldn't be seen or felt, but I forced myself to stay put. Our eyes were locked. She whispered something urgent in Creole. I didn't understand, but I was sure she asked for help. I was afraid to touch her—partly because I thought I'd hurt her and partly because I was afraid of catching whatever it was that she had. I should have taken those gloves.

Thankfully, the doctor came back in the room and walked over to her cot. He nodded hello to me and then knelt by the woman, quietly talking to her as he carefully peeled back the sheet to examine her. She cried out in agony. I held my breath as I looked at her skin. Her whole body was covered in sores. She was bald. Maybe she'd been burned. As he gently wrapped her back up, I heard him say to his assistant that she had some kind of skin disease. Untreatable at Son Fils. There was nothing they could do.

The rest of the morning passed slowly. I felt the weight of every minute. Why did she have to suffer like this? Couldn't she be put out of her misery, either with painkillers or—I wasn't sure I should even think it—with death? What's the point of someone suffering so much without hope or help? I thought of how quickly Rich died. Five minutes. This woman had been suffering for days, months, maybe her whole life, and who knew how long she'd live?

As I watched her try to sleep, I noticed that the sheet she was wrapped in had a butterfly pattern. It wasn't white like all the others. Printed all over it were blue butterflies, yellow butterflies, pink butterflies. She was wrapped in butterflies—my favorite sign of hope and transformation. How ironic. Where was her hope? She was left on her cot to peel away, one piece of skin at a time.

I stared at her sheet, wondering if there was a message hidden in it for her or for me. My thoughts drifted to the days after Rich's funeral, when butterflies were my comfort. They became a sign of God's presence in my grief, appearing frequently outside my kitchen window and at Rich's gravesite. I even discovered one inside my home. Now butterflies were in Son Fils. But did she feel God's presence? At that moment, I didn't.

Beads of sweat rolled down my forehead. The heat and stale air started to get to me. I held my stomach, afraid I might throw up. As I watched her shiver and moan, my body started to tremble too, with anger that rose to my throat. I wanted to scream—at God, at the world.

That night, I couldn't sleep. Wrapped in my own sheet, I cried in the darkness and prayed for help—for the butterfly woman, the mother of three, the woman who wanted to brush her teeth, the residents of Cité Soleil, and all the children. Their situation was so overwhelming, I felt weighed down with a sense of hopelessness. Suddenly, in the silence of the night, my head filled with the singing of morning prayers at Son Fils. I heard the deep, rich voice of the butterfly woman. I pulled my sheet tightly around me and shuddered as I thought of her peeling skin and sores. But her singing, her voice. In it was a strength and power that called out from her dark cocoon and clung fiercely to life. I felt how deeply she had looked into my eyes, how urgently she'd whispered something. She hadn't given up hope, and as I thought about her wrapped in her butterfly sheet, whispering to me, I heard her urging me not to give up either.

Father Gerry

His hearty laugh filled the hotel courtyard. Laughter had been rare on our trip. The sound of it was quite refreshing and instantly made me smile. I looked up and saw our evening speaker, Father Gérard Jean-Juste, also known as Fr. Gerry, standing on the balcony. He was the priest of St. Clare's Church, where we'd worshipped a few days earlier. I remembered the packed pews and his powerful presence as he led the congregation in the St. Jude prayer. I was looking forward to hearing him speak.

Each night after volunteering at Son Fils, our group gathered to hear a guest speaker discuss aspects of Haiti's culture, spirituality, and history. We also learned about development programs that were working: a bank, called Fonkoze, that gave microloans to groups of women who wanted to start their own businesses. Reforestation projects in the countryside. A bakery in a rural town that helped the residents become self-sufficient. A solar cooking project that helped Haitians move away from charcoal fuel. These evening sessions were a good balance to the intensity of the rest of the day.

I settled into one of the chairs arranged in a circle on the open-air balcony. The evening was warm and breezy. I immediately felt drawn to Fr. Gerry's energy and smile. He was in his early 50s and was dressed in a short-sleeved white shirt and black pants, with a pink rosary around his neck. He exuded joy and confidence. Bryan introduced him, saying that he grew up in Cavaillon, a coastal village in southern Haiti. His parents were impoverished farmers. When he was a teenager, friends made it possible for him to go to Canada so he could work his way through school and then seminary near Montréal. He always wanted to be a priest. After graduation, he served the Haitian community in Brooklyn and became the first Haitian Catholic priest ordained in the United States. With the help of a scholarship named after Martin Luther King Jr., he received a civil engineering degree from Northeastern University in Boston. He later moved to "Little Haiti" in northeast Miami and served as Executive Director of the Haitian Refugee Center, advocating for the rights of Haitian refugees who were fleeing the Duvalier regime.

After "Baby Doc" Duvalier fled Haiti, Fr. Gerry returned to Port-au-Prince. His sparkling eyes revealed a love for his country and a hope for its future.

Throughout the evening, Fr. Gerry talked about the struggle of the Haitian people for democracy, human rights, and basic services. He talked about the vast inequities in Haiti and throughout the world and was passionate about the needs and rights of the poor. His charismatic presence drew us in. There was something about him that elicited trust and hope. I could sense his strong leadership and his ability to make things happen. I could understand why the pews were packed on Sundays and knew that's where I would attend church if I lived in Haiti. He described how he "saw" the roads paved, the people fed, employed, healthy, educated, and housed. He believed in a future for Haiti's children and was committed to help make it happen.

At the end of his talk, a member of our group asked about the extent of hunger in Haiti. He paused and quietly described Sunday mornings at St. Clare's Church. "Every week, the children come to me. They point to their bellies and then their lips. 'My Father, do you have any food in your cupboard for me to eat?' I give them what I can, but it is not close to enough. I have a vision for a food program for the hungry children in my community."

These words touched something inside me. Maybe it was a knowing. Or a "call." But I instantly felt a part of me leap at his vision of a food program. From head to toe, my body tingled with energy. My heartbeat quickened. Throughout the trip, Bryan had told us not to rush into the "What can I do to fix this?" mentality. Instead he continued to remind us to allow our experience to open our hearts. As we explored the feelings that surfaced and looked deeply into our faith, the answers about how to respond would reveal themselves. I felt that my answer had revealed itself right there on the balcony.

When I left Haiti two days later, the despair I'd felt after my day with the butterfly lady had started to lift. The possibility of finding a way to respond to what I'd experienced at Son Fils and Cité Soleil captured my heart and gave me hope.

Reentry

The Miami airport was like another world—clean, carpeted, air-conditioned, with toilets that flushed and the smell of fresh donuts and coffee. It was a welcome sight, familiar and comfortable. But it was also disturbing. I watched well-dressed passengers hurry through the airport on their way to Caribbean destinations carrying cell phones and laptops, fast food and lattes. Healthy toddlers holding toys and sippy cups in their strollers contrasted with the children I'd seen in Cité Soleil playing in the dirt. I doubted that anyone in the airport had any idea what was happening on one of the islands they were about to fly over on their way to their vacation. I wanted to scream, "HELP! There's an emergency and it's only a few hundred miles from here. We have to do something, change something. Quick. People are dying!"

Everywhere I looked there were stores filled with clothes, toiletries, magazines, toys, and food!—burgers and ice cream, burritos and grilled cheese. Food and more food—food everywhere. Half-eaten sandwiches left in the waiting area. Garbage cans stuffed with wrappers and unfinished meals. Kids too full to finish their Happy Meals. I thought of the mothers in Cité Soleil. I was relieved to be back in the States, where the comforts and convenience and abundance overflowed. But at the same time, I felt nauseated.

When I got home and jumped back into my daily routine of carpooling, laundry, work, and taking care of Luke, the fast pace of my life consumed me. I raced from one thing to the next, but the women at Son Fils and the people in Cité Soleil were never far from my thoughts. At every meal, and especially when I scraped food we were too full to finish into the garbage or threw out wilted lettuce I never got around to eating, I remembered the children on the street saying "M'grangou," and Fr. Gerry's vision. I saw their faces, the eyes of the mother of three and the butterfly lady—but I was so far away, and I didn't know what I could do from such a distance.

Shortly after I got back, I went to Costco to buy some things for an ice cream social at Luke's school. I hadn't been there in ages, and I'd forgotten how massive it is. Rows and rows and rows of supersized cereal, candy, chips, and soda, everything in bulk. I wheeled my cart through the aisles, struck by the fact that most of the food on the shelves had no nutritional value. It was luxury food, fun food, unhealthy food. I wondered how much money I spent on food that offered no benefit to my body. I was sure it had to be hundreds, if not thousands, of dollars a year.

The cashier rang up the ice cream, hot fudge, and whipped cream for the school social and then the strip of AA batteries for Luke's Game Boy, a case of sparkling water, a gigantic bag of chocolate chips, blank videos, and other things I'd thrown in the cart for my home. When she processed my credit card, I knew I could have fed dozens and dozens of children for the same amount.

I couldn't ignore my discomfort with the consumerism I was so much a part of. I felt restless and guilty, but not sure how to address my feelings about the difference between my life and the lives of those I'd seen in Port-au-Prince. Like the women with the cotton ball, I knew I had to discover what was enough for me and Luke—enough food, enough clothes, enough toys, enough stuff. My closets were packed with pants and tops I didn't wear. My refrigerator was filled with food I didn't eat. Luke's shelves overflowed with toys he didn't play with. My house was bursting with excess. I decided to go through it all, clean it out, and give away everything I didn't use or love.

When I shopped at the grocery store, every time I reached for something, I paused to think about whether it would actually be eaten or would end up in my garbage or on my shelf until it expired. Whenever I passed a homeless person on the street, I stopped, made an effort to look them in the eye, and took the time to reach into my purse for a dollar. Giving felt so much better than ignoring.

But the feeling of restlessness continued.

One night, a recurring nightmare woke me up. It was a dream I had once or twice a year during times of stress—tornadoes swirling toward me from all directions, threatening to blow me away. Sweaty and trembling, I lay awake until dawn thinking about how the shade that had once separated me from the suffering of the world had been blown away as a result of the "reverse mission." I couldn't reenter my life as it was—all about me and Luke. My heart wouldn't close up. It ached, and it pleaded for a response.

As I lay in bed thinking about Haiti, images of Fr. Gerry and his church, the boy who collapsed, the prayer to St. Jude, and the S.O.S. that had been spelled out by the elderly lady with the fan played over and over in my mind. The images didn't haunt me. They called to me.

Another Sign

I shared Fr. Gerry's vision of a food program with my parents the next day. I thought my dad might have ideas about how to get churches involved or how to start something when you're thousands of miles away. We brainstormed, but didn't come up with anything concrete.

Shortly after we hung up, my dad called back. He'd just been to his office and had opened the day's mail. A few weeks earlier, his church conference had sent a grant for $5,000 to a food pantry. As the conference president, he had just received a letter notifying him that the pantry had closed. The check was returned—unused. Since it was intended for hunger relief, he said it was possible to redirect the money to Haiti.

I listened with amazement. This must be a sign! A huge weight lifted off my heart and, elated, I danced around my kitchen. Five thousand dollars! I called Bryan to get Fr. Gerry's e-mail address and wrote him immediately, explaining that I had met him on the hotel balcony, had heard him describe his vision for a food program for the hungry children in his community, and that I wanted to help him make this a reality. He wrote back a few days later, elated as well and already in action. He said the food program would be ready to begin when the check arrived. Dad mailed the check and we waited.

March 26, 2000

Dear Margaret,

The program is wonderful! I just want to let you know that it is working beautifully. From 200 participants last Sunday, it has doubled today. We have been called to a big assignment from God in feeding the hungry brothers and sisters. The news is being spread. Children and their needy parents are pouring on us. I use many volunteers. Many youngsters want to help. I am using the rectory quarters. I need more chairs, more tables, more food, more of everything. The supervisor of the program is a great woman who loves this volunteer task. There is great hope. Now I am exhausted. It is getting late. It is too much, too exciting to count and report all now. God certainly has talked to you today while we were implementing this great inspiration . . .

Best regards to you and all,
Gerry

The speed of the food program's birth astounded me. I'd been home from Haiti just two months. Fr. Gerry had just received the $5,000 check and already he had lined up the cooks, bought plates and forks, announced the good news, and begun. He told me that food was being purchased from the local farmers' market, helping to support the Haitian economy. The cost of each meal was about fifty cents.

Inspired, I shared his e-mail with my friends, and a few checks started to arrive in my mailbox. Ten dollars, $25, $100. I told each person that every dollar fed two children.

I wasn't sure what I was getting into or where it would lead. Things seemed to have a life of their own, and I felt swept along for the ride. But my heart felt full and happy, and so I didn't worry.

Dear Margaret,

The children are happy. We served more than 400 today. Good menu. Nothing left. God's blessing for all of us, always, everywhere ...

Dear Margaret,

Jesus is happy we're implementing one of his main teachings: Feed his people. My team and I love it. We work hard to feed some 400 needy children on Sundays. Let's hope we can institutionalize this for generations to come...

Dear Margaret,

You should hear what they say about the hot meal they receive on Sundays. They say that Sunday is the best day of the week. They cannot wait to have Sunday. Sunday is too far away sometimes for those who are hungry.

I kept spreading the word, friend to friend. More checks arrived. I opened a separate bank account and started thinking about the need to create a nonprofit organization. I had no idea how to do this, but I was sure I knew someone who knew someone who knew how.

Weeks passed quickly. Every Sunday, I pictured the food program, imagining the dishes of hot food and the smiles on the faces of the children. With each e-mail from Fr. Gerry, I longed to return, to see the meals being served, if only for a few days. I e-mailed Father Gerry that I wanted to visit, and he wrote back that he had arranged for me to stay with members of his congregation. He'd meet me at the airport. Come anytime.

My parents were nervous about me returning to Haiti alone, so they bought a plane ticket for my younger brother, Paul. We are good friends, so I was thrilled to have his company. Paul was a self-employed artist who lived simply in a 500-square-foot cabin on the outskirts of Sonoma, California. He was just scraping by, selling a painting here and there. He jumped at the chance to go.

We left for Haiti in July, seven months after my first visit. As promised, Father Gerry greeted us at the airport. I wasn't as scared this time.

PART II

Like welcoming a long-lost daughter home

"Welcome Home"

As we exited the airport, we drove past the thick crowd of men waiting for the opportunity to carry someone's suitcase. I remembered how overwhelmed I'd felt the first time I landed. This visit felt different.

"I have the perfect place for you to stay," Fr. Gerry said as we inched along the rugged streets in his jeep. We'd only exchanged a couple of e-mails about my visit, and the details of living arrangements hadn't been mentioned. All I knew was that Paul and I would be staying with members of his congregation. "You'll be with a wonderful family. They are waiting for you."

It took about ten minutes to get to the neighborhood of St. Clare's. I'd been there once before, for Mass. The passionate prayer to St. Jude came to mind as we bounced in and out of potholes. The area looked like the rest of Port-au-Prince, run-down and without basic services like running water or electricity. Most homes were sparsely furnished one- or two-room concrete-block structures. There were no sidewalks or grassy lawns—just a few scraggly trees. Tiny shops and merchant stalls lined the main street, selling tires, canned goods, mangoes, fabric, charcoal. I spotted a barber shop without walls, with a man getting his hair trimmed under the sun.

Half a mile from the church, we turned left down a dusty road. Fr. Gerry expertly maneuvered around boulders and a family of goats and pulled into the dirt driveway of our host family—the Dépestres. They were at the heart of the food program, Fr. Gerry told us, devoting every Saturday and Sunday to the project since it had started in March.

When I stepped out of the car, a woman in her early 70s rose from her rocking chair and walked toward us, waving. She wore a bright-orange patterned blouse with a green-and-white skirt. Her silky black hair was pulled back in two braids that wound into a bun. She walked toward me with her arms outstretched and kissed me on both cheeks. "Welcome home, Margo," she said warmly, looking into my eyes and smiling broadly. Her words gave me goose bumps. Welcome home—what a beautiful greeting. And I already had a nickname. I'd always been "Margaret."

Fr. Gerry introduced her—she was Manmi Dèt. He explained that *manmi* meant "mother" in Creole. Odette was her first name. She was called Manmi Dèt because she was regarded as the mother of the community. Everyone loved her.

As Paul gathered our bags, Manmi Dèt put her arm around me and led me up freshly painted red stairs to a bedroom. I waved to Fr. Gerry, who was backing out of the driveway. He'd just dropped my brother and me off with a complete stranger, but I wasn't worried. I felt comfortable with Manmi Dèt. I could feel warmth and love radiate right out of her, like the nun I'd met at Son Fils.

Her house had five small rooms that she shared with her son, daughter-in-law, and granddaughter. It was about 1,000 square feet, much larger than most of the homes we passed. Manmi Dèt's other children, including her daughter Nennenn, the food program's chief cook, had their own houses just a few yards away. Manmi Dèt knew a tiny bit of English, so we communicated mostly with smiles and hand gestures.

"Yours, Margo," she said as she opened the door to one of the rooms. In it were two neatly made beds covered with thin brown bedspreads. There was also an orange plastic chair, an old wooden dresser, and a bureau. She led me to the adjoining bathroom and pointed to the sink. "No water." She frowned, turning the faucet handle all the way around. I nodded. She pointed to a large bucket of water and a sponge. Sponge baths. Then she scooped out a small container full of water and poured it down the toilet. It was a weak flush, but it flushed! She smiled, and I clapped in relief.

Even though it was clear that Manmi Dèt was well-off compared to most Haitians, by U.S. standards she lived very simply. She didn't have a phone or a washing machine or air-conditioning or a couch. There were large cracks in the walls, and the brown jeep in her driveway was old and rusted. I was worried we might be a burden, but she put me at ease. She joyfully handed me the keys and said, "Your home."

After helping me unpack, Manmi Dèt smoothed the bedspreads and motioned for me to come with her. She took my hand and led me down the stairs to a small kitchen under the bedroom. Mismatched cups and plates were stacked neatly on a shelf. In the center of the room was a wooden table covered with a red plastic tablecloth and four chairs.

"Hungry?" she asked.

"No, *merci.*" I said, not wanting to eat unless she ate.

She poured me a glass of bottled water and led me to the porch. Paul joined us. One by one, family members stopped by to say hello. Manmi Dèt proudly introduced us, never letting go of my hand.

When Paul and I turned in for the night, we discovered a tray of rice and beans waiting for us on the dresser. A plastic cover was placed over each plate to keep the flies away. Fresh-squeezed juice filled two glasses. We sat on our beds and dug in, hungrier than we'd thought. Suddenly the electricity went off. My heart skipped a beat, and for a second, thoughts of a possible coup d'état or burglars filled my mind. Looking out the window, we could see that the whole neighborhood was pitch black. But then I heard Manmi Dèt through the grate in the wall chatting and laughing with her family. My concerns faded as I listened to her move effortlessly around the house in the dark. Just another power outage.

Roosters crowed, dogs barked, babies cried—the sounds of night filled the room. Under my pale blue sheet, as I lay awake, thinking about the events of the day, I felt surprisingly relaxed and present. The frenzy with which I wrapped up work, packed, and drove to the airport the day before seemed a distant memory. The frantic pace of my life in Berkeley somehow vanished as soon as I got into Fr. Gerry's jeep. I fell asleep thinking about Manmi Dèt.

Meeting her was one of those rare and wonderful times when I felt as if I'd been reunited with someone I'd known forever. We spoke only a few words to each other, but the way she held my hand and smiled when she looked at me— it was like a mother welcoming a long-lost daughter home.

St. Clare's

F r. Gerry leaned out his car window and pointed to the peach-colored church sitting on a hill a few blocks in front of us. "Look at the roof, Margaret and Paul. Could you see what we painted on it when your plane landed yesterday? You flew right over us."

I hadn't noticed the church from the plane, but now that I could see its roof, I wondered how I missed it. In gigantic blue and red block letters (the colors of the Haitian flag) "St. Clare's" was spelled out for all to see—from the planes above to the entire neighborhood.

"It's fantastic! Isn't it?" Fr. Gerry exclaimed as he admired his creative advertising. "Now everyone who comes to Haiti will know where to find us. ST. CLA-A-A-A-RE, ST. CLA-A-A-A-RE," he called out. An elderly lady sweeping her front stoop looked up at the sound of his voice and waved as we chugged by. He said something back to her, and they both laughed. He seemed to know everyone in the area.

"Bonjou, mon pè!" (Hello, Father.) A dozen boys stopped their game of basketball to greet us as we pulled in front of the church.

"See the new hoop I got for the children? They stay close now, so I can keep an eye on them." Fr. Gerry chatted and joked with the boys, who were thrilled with their new metal rim and pole.

"And look at our bell tower, Margaret. It's on its way." The "tower" sat to the left of the church building. It was only 3 feet tall. I assumed lack of funds had temporarily stalled the project. Even though it was far from complete, it looked beautiful. Cream-colored rocks of various sizes were carefully arranged to fit together like a mosaic. "We've made lots of improvements since you were here in January. We also have two fans and a new microphone. Someday we'll have air-conditioning. Oh, the congregation will love that! Come inside."

Paul and I followed down the center aisle. The sanctuary, with its white tile floor, butter-colored walls, and blue-tinted windows, seemed much bigger and brighter than I remembered it. I guessed that the pews held at least 700 people. A sexton nodded hello from behind the lectern. He was coiling microphone wires and arranging chairs for afternoon Mass. As I walked down the aisle, my mind replayed the scene from my only other visit to St. Clare's—the time when the little boy collapsed right in front of me during the service. The thought sent a shiver up my spine.

Today the plain wooden pews were empty except for an occasional Bible or songbook. In the front of the church, three steps led to a communion table draped with a white tablecloth. A vase filled with purple and yellow plastic flowers was placed on it. On the front wall was a crucifix, a picture of Mary, and a small white statue of St. Clare. As I approached the communion table, a gentle breeze blew through the open doors. With the sun streaming in and with its airy, fresh feeling, I imagined St. Clare's provided a welcome respite for its parishioners.

"We're repainting the saints." Fr. Gerry pointed to twelve glass window paintings that were positioned side by side, up high on the front wall of the church. I could make out the shadow of an artist who was painting one of the panes of glass in a second-floor room just behind the paintings. "Right now, we're working on St. Luke. His glass cracked, so we have a brand-new piece." I was surprised at the European look of the saints—just like my picture books from Sunday School. They seemed out of place in the sanctuary, and I wondered if the artist was making any changes to St. Luke's face and hair.

As we looked up at the paintings, Paul casually mentioned to Fr. Gerry that he was an artist, too.

"You're an artist? That's fantastic!" Fr. Gerry's eyes sparkled. He put his arm around Paul and pointed to the back wall. "Tell me what you think about the balcony, Paul. Just this week I had an idea." He paused and rubbed his chin. "We need something on that back yellow wall. I was thinking that a risen Christ would look perfect there, don't you?"

Paul nodded in agreement.

Fr. Gerry held up his hand, moving it from side to side as if measuring the imaginary painting. I could see that it was already complete in his mind. "This is perfect timing! You're an artist. You can do it. We'll get you some paint and you can paint this weekend, okay?"

Paul looked stunned. "But Father Gerry, I've never painted anything that big before. I'm an oil-on-canvas painter. It usually takes me over a year to finish a small painting, and I'm only here four more days."

Paul had a good point. He'd been working on the same paintings for years. I loved his work. It was always worth the wait. It was Renaissance style, usually with a spiritual theme. Jesus was in several of his paintings. But Paul was definitely not a painter who cranked things out. He seemed to obsess over the tiniest details. The process seemed almost painful to him. His pace and the fact that he hated marketing his work made it tough for him to make a living as an artist. But from his talent, it seemed clear that he was born to paint.

My eyes moved back and forth between Paul and Father Gerry. I hoped Paul would say yes. A gigantic Jesus at St. Clare's—what an amazing opportunity!

Still staring at the blank wall, Fr. Gerry smiled and said, "No problem, Paul. Whatever you do will be great."

Paul glanced at me, a look of concern in his eyes, and I nodded encouragingly. "Well . . . maybe I can do an outline . . . . And then another artist can finish it. Do you have a piece of chalk?"

Fr. Gerry called out to a young boy who was peeking through the side door. He dashed off and returned with a piece of charcoal and a wooden ladder. It was as easy as that. In a matter of seconds, Paul had his assignment for the weekend.

As Fr. Gerry and Paul talked about the painting, I wondered what my assignment would be for the weekend. Normally, I planned out every detail of a business trip, complete with a typed agenda neatly placed in a folder. But I didn't know where to start with Fr. Gerry and the food program. That morning's visit to St. Clare's was a surprise. So was the painting. I had no idea what we were going to do next. I could sense that asking for details wasn't appropriate. Fr. Gerry seemed to operate on another level—as if he was following inspiration, not an agenda. I decided that my plan was to have no plan and simply follow Fr. Gerry's lead.

"Margaret and Paul. This is Berry Philippe." Berry shook our hands enthusiastically. He looked about 12 and was dressed in a faded gray T-shirt, shorts, and plastic flip-flops that were too big for him. "Berry's one of my altar boys. He's a great helper. He will stay with you, Paul, so you can get started. Margaret and I will be back later, after we go to the paint store."

Leave Paul behind? I wasn't so sure about this idea. We'd promised Mom and Dad we'd stick together. What if something happened when we were gone? I was pretty sure Berry didn't speak a word of English. Before I could offer another suggestion, Father Gerry's cell phone rang and he stepped outside.

"I'll be fine, Margaret. Don't worry." Paul said, as he and Berry lugged the ladder up the winding metal staircase to the balcony. I could see Paul was starting to get excited about painting Jesus.

I held my breath as I watched Paul slowly climb to the top of the ladder, testing each step to make sure it wouldn't break. The ladder looked ancient. Its steps were loose, held together by rusted nails. It wasn't a stepladder; it just leaned against the wall. I was sure it would slip to one side or the other if it weren't for Berry, who braced his body against the bottom legs of the ladder, holding it in place. When Paul got to the top, his six-foot-two-inch body looked tiny against the huge yellow wall.

Fr. Gerry honked the horn, signaling it was time to go. "Are you sure you're going to be okay?" I whispered, looking over my shoulder as I walked down the stairs. Paul smiled and waved me on. He looked calm and confident. I felt that way, too, even though I knew I should probably be more worried or at least more careful. I couldn't explain it, but something about St. Clare's gave me a feeling of safety. Of course, being "PKs" (pastor's kids), Paul and I felt at home in a church. But it was more than that. Maybe it was the friendly sexton, or young Berry, or the daisy-colored balcony wall. Or maybe I'd started to change. The feeling of being over-whelmed that I had experienced throughout my first visit to Haiti had faded to the background. Miserable conditions sur-rounded me, but the food program was on Sunday, and with Fr. Gerry and Manmi Dèt I felt hopeful and excited about what was possible.

Miracles

Bumping down the hill to the paint store, I started to re-gret not giving Paul Fr. Gerry's cell phone number. I pictured him teetering on the top of the ladder. What if he fell and broke an arm or leg? What if he was kidnapped? Someone back home had warned me of kidnappings. "You never know ...," they said, ominously. I brushed these fears aside, reminding myself that I felt safer in the Tiplas Kazo neighborhood than in certain parts of Berkeley. Plus, violence throughout Haiti had dropped to a tiny fraction of what it had been before the Aristide and Préval governments. It was a good time to be there.

I reached into my bag for my notebook and pen. I'd cre-ated a long list of questions for Fr. Gerry. Some were weighty—thoughts that had been troubling me since my first visit to Haiti. Even though I barely knew him, I felt I could ask him anything. This was the perfect opportunity for a pri-vate conversation. So, right there in the jeep as it pitched and creaked along—I started in on my most pressing question:

"How is it, Father Gerry, that Haitian people have such a deep faith in God? When there's so little food and few jobs and no doctors or running water, I'd think that after a while, a person might reject the idea of God, or at least a loving and just God."

He smiled. I could tell he liked this question.

"God is the first and the last resource here. We feel God's presence more and more, because there is nobody else some days who can sustain us to allow us to survive. It's only God sometimes." He paused to drive around a stalled car. "Because the neighbor doesn't have enough, the friends don't have anything, so we're praising God. God makes miracles. So we live by miracles, and as we live by miracles, we need faith. Our faith sustains us."

He beeped his horn and waved at the people standing along the road. *"Ki jan w ye?"* (How are you?) he called out. *"Pa pi mal"* (Not bad), they responded, smiling and waving. I wrote his answer down quickly in my notebook, trying to understand the depth of what he was saying.

"You will observe that wherever there is a lot of misery, there is less suicide." I looked up, surprised at where this question was taking us. Suicide was not on my list. "The suicide rate is very low in Haiti. Poor people don't kill themselves. They always have hope. Something, something is coming."

He was quiet for a minute, and so was I. I looked out my window at the rows and rows of dilapidated homes. Stagnant water pools full of garbage baked in the heat. The smell was nauseating.

"In the midst of trouble, the presence of God is felt more and more," he said softly.

That had definitely been my experience after Rich's death. When I was really struggling, my whole understanding of God shifted—from a God far away to a God close, present with me in my darkest hour. But I felt uncomfortable making comparisons between my life and the life of Haitians. I'd been through a very painful time, but the worst of it had passed. The people I saw outside the car window had a life-long struggle with the basic necessities of life. They'd lived not only through the deaths of spouses, but the deaths of children, siblings, parents, and friends. They'd lived through coups, brutal military regimes, devastating hurricanes, and drought. I was visiting during a relatively peaceful moment in Haiti's political history. The country was preparing for another presidential election as Préval's term ended. Jean-Bertrand Aristide was running again and had the support of the masses. He was expected to win by a landslide. Fr. Gerry said that the country was hopeful that his election would bring new schools, hospitals, and cooperatives. Still, life seemed miserable for most Haitians. I didn't know if I would be able to have hope and belief in a loving God if I lived under these conditions.

We turned onto Jean-Jacques Dessalines Boulevard, the main road in downtown Port-au-Prince, named after a leader of the Haitian Revolution and the first ruler of independent Haiti. Gridlock surrounded us. A woman drenched in sweat, balancing a large basket of fruit on her head, with buckets of water in each hand, walked in front of us. The muscles on her shoulders and arms were well defined, her posture straight, her walk graceful. She looked my age.

"It's a matter of every day surviving." Fr. Gerry suddenly continued. "So, every day, we expect God will make miracles. And indeed He does. I've met some families, and I don't know how they feed themselves. People eat whenever they find food. They drink whenever they find water. Suppose there is a party someplace. When we go to parties, we fill our plates like a pyramid in case it is a long time before we eat again."

"So each time they find food, it's considered a miracle from God?" I asked.

He nodded.

I watched the wall-to-wall street vendors we passed, wondering if they'd experience a miracle that day. An exchange of a mango for a bowl of rice? A piece of chicken for a yard of cloth? Up until that moment, I'd always thought of miracles as rare and mysterious events you might miss if you weren't watching closely. I'd counted only a handful in my life experiences. Eating a meal had not been one of them. But that $5,000 check? That was a miracle.

And now I was beginning to understand how a plate of food is just as much a miracle.

Paint for Jezi

After two hours of inching through Port-au-Prince traffic, Father Gerry pulled over and parked on a congested street in the shopping district to buy paint. The buildings were simple, but they were packed with stores featuring imported appliances, expensive furniture, televisions, and stereos. There were shops displaying colorful party dresses and hats. Shoe stores with the latest styles. One of the storefront windows had a mannequin dressed in a flowing, white-lace bridal dress. Who had the money to buy all this stuff? Then I remembered the tiny percentage of wealthy Haitians who lived in the villas on the hills overlooking Port-au-Prince.

When we entered the small fine arts store, Fr. Gerry casually asked what type of paint Paul needed. I stopped and gulped, looking at rows and rows of paint. It hadn't occurred to me to ask Paul this obvious question before we left. I didn't have a clue. Fr. Gerry laughed that hearty laugh I'd heard at the hotel months earlier. He walked up to the sales clerk and explained the project.

"What colors, Margaret?"

"Ah . . . White and black," I guessed.

"Rouge et verte aussi," Fr. Gerry added. Red and green. We left the store a few minutes later with one paintbrush and four tubes of paint.

By midafternoon, we were back at St. Clare's. Paul and Berry Philippe were on the front steps watching a half-court basketball game. The outline was finished! Paul, himself amazed, described how it had practically drawn itself. He'd started with the eyes. Standing on the top step of the ladder, inches from the wall, without a tape measure, sketch, or grid, he guessed where the right eye should go. Because the wall was so big, he only knew that he'd guessed right after he climbed down the ladder, went down the spiral steps, walked to the front of the church, and looked back at the wall. The right eye was in the perfect place. It was the perfect size. Then he walked back to draw the left eye. Another guess. Perfect. Back and forth all afternoon, checking every stroke he made. Each one was in perfect proportion. At this rate, he said, he might finish the whole painting over the weekend.

Paul and Berry led the way up the balcony's creaky spiral staircase to show us the outline. Jesus was huge—at least 15 feet tall. His waist started at the floor and the top of his head hit the ceiling. He was naked, with a slash at his ribs and round holes in his hands. His arms were outstretched, as if embracing the congregation. He had a wide nose, long thick black hair, and a beard. He looked like many of the other Jesuses Paul had painted over the years.

Father Gerry stared at the outline in silence for what seemed like ages. Maybe he expected a blond-haired, blue-eyed, ivory-skinned Jesus. Not one who looked Middle Eastern or Hispanic or Haitian.

"I can make changes if you want, Father Gerry," Paul said.

Still silence. Then finally, "No, Paul. I like it. I like it." He walked from one side of the balcony to the other, never taking

his eyes off Jesus. Then he added, "There's only one thing."
He paused. "Can you put a robe or cloth on him?"

"No problem." Paul smiled, relieved.

I handed Paul the bag of paints. White, black, red, green,
he pulled them out and placed them on the pew. They were
the right kind and the right colors.

"Is there yellow?" Paul whispered so Fr. Gerry couldn't
hear.

"Why do you need yellow? The whole wall is yellow," I
whispered back.

"In case I make a mistake." I hadn't thought about that.
Paul smiled, looking a little concerned. "No mistakes."

Paul pulled the one brush we'd bought out of the bag. "Is
this the only brush?"

I nodded, realizing it was much too small for the job. In
that tiny paint store, I'd forgotten how huge the wall was. He
needed the kind of brush you paint a house with. "Sorry." I
whispered.

"This'll work. I think." Paul smiled. "Thank you, Father
Gerry, for the supplies." Fr. Gerry was still staring at Jesus.

Berry Philippe and Paul got back to work. They made a
great team. Paul squeezed paint from each tube onto his
palette—a small section of cardboard—and climbed back up
the ladder. It creaked with each step. With Paul balancing on
the top step, Berry slowly let go of the ladder's legs, picked
up the cardboard, climbed on a pew he'd positioned next
to Paul, and held it over his head. Berry was the perfect
height so Paul didn't have to lean too far to dip his brush. As
I left the church for Manmi Dèt's house, I thought if we got
through the weekend without an accident, and with enough
paint, it would be another Haitian miracle.

Poudre d'Amour

When Fr. Gerry dropped me off at Manmi Dèt's, preparations for the Sunday food program had already begun. It was only Friday, but Manmi Dèt's daughter Nennenn, who was in charge of the meal, had something special in mind.

After changing out of my sweat-drenched clothes, I walked down a rocky path to Nennenn's to help. She lived only 25 yards from Manmi Dèt in a rectangular cement house. "*Bonjou,* Margo," Nennenn called, waving from her red iron door. She was dressed in a checked muumuu and had a bright red scarf wrapped around her head. "We're making a treat for the children. Come inside."

The sweet smell of coconut filled her kitchen. Nennenn lifted a heavy pot full of what looked like Granola off the burner and put it on the table. "It's good. Try some." She put a spoonful in my hand and motioned for me to lick it off, watching me eagerly, awaiting my reaction. Coconut, sugar, butter, maybe some oats. Delicious! Crunchy.

"This is for Sunday?"

"Yes," she said with her expressive, happy eyes, and a big smile. She had a ton of energy. I guessed she was in her mid- to late 40s. I was thrilled she spoke English.

Nennenn's 12-year-old adopted daughter, Nancy, came into the room and greeted me with a shy smile and a kiss on the cheek. Nennenn said that Nancy's mother, a good friend of hers, had died a few years ago and Nancy had lived with her since then. Nennenn had three other children—two were students in Cuba. Her son Kiko was getting a degree in mathematics. Her daughter, Romi, was a first-year medical student. Her other son, Luigi, worked in a furniture store downtown. Her husband had died of cancer.

Nennenn worked full-time as a high school administrator. She'd taken the afternoon off to cook up the coconut dessert. I guessed from the simplicity of her home that she spent most of her income on her children's tuition. The walls were unpainted. The main room had only one table and three chairs. When I went to use her bathroom, I peeked in her bedroom and saw that it had a dresser covered with pictures of her children and a mattress on the floor.

Nancy placed a pile of tiny plastic bags in the middle of the empty living room and sat down cross-legged with a bowl of the treat and a spoon. I was surprised to see that she was planning to spoon the coconut mixture into each of the 500 bags, one for each child. It seemed like an overwhelming task that could take hours.

Nennenn turned on the radio, immersing the room with hip-shaking Haitian music, handed me a spoon, smiling, and pointed to the pot. I sat down next to Nancy on the tile floor, and we got to work. Three spoonfuls filled a bag and left room at the top for a knot, which Manmi Dèt volunteered to tie. Manmi Dèt pulled up a wicker chair next to where I was sitting, and I handed her my first bag. One down, 499 to go. The room was hot and muggy. Mosquitoes were circling. I had a hard time sitting still and wondered if there wasn't an easier way to do this. How about spooning it into each child's hands, or placing big bowls of it on each table at the end of the meal? I imagined the scene and decided that this was definitely not a good idea.

Nancy and Manmi Dèt chatted happily in Creole, obviously enjoying the project. Nennenn danced between the pots, tasting and stirring, adding sugar and vanilla when needed. I was clearly the only one thinking about time and efficiency issues.

"Tell me about the food program, Nennenn," I said. "It must be a lot of work to prepare all the food."

"Yes. It takes time." She smiled as she stirred and shook her hips to the music.

"And you volunteer?" I knew the answer to this, but asked anyway because part of me couldn't believe she'd give such a huge chunk of her time every weekend. Especially since she worked full-time and had Nancy to raise.

"Yes. I do . . . Because I love the children."

"How long does the meal usually take to prepare?"

"All day Saturday. And Sunday until two or three, because the pots need to be washed."

She seemed unfazed by this, but I counted up the hours. I thought of week after week after week—sixteen weeks so far since the first meal was served in March. And this weekend, she'd added the work of shredding coconuts. Plus, the hours of bag-spooning.

As I scooped and sweated, settling into the monotonous task, I looked at each bag and thought of the hungry child it represented. Thanks to the patience and heart of these women, the children would have the choice of opening their bags and pouring the delicious contents immediately into their mouths. Or maybe they'd choose to sprinkle the coconut chunks into the palms of their hands. Or they might take their treats home and savor them bit by bit.

"What's the name of this dessert, Nennenn?" I asked, as I crunched on another handful. It was addictive.

"*Poudre d'amour.*"

Powder of love.

The Market

I heard a gentle beep on the horn, signaling it was time to leave for the market. Toto, one of Fr. Gerry's assistants, had arrived to pick us up. He and Nennenn went to the downtown Port-au-Prince farmers' market every Saturday morning to buy the food needed for Sunday's meal. We threw empty vegetable sacks into the backseat of the jeep and climbed in.

As we backed out of her driveway, Nennenn counted the money Fr. Gerry had given her for the meal. She recorded everything she bought and how much it cost in a Mickey Mouse spiral notebook. I thumbed through it and saw page after page of notes. Garlic, carrots, cabbage, beans, rice, chicken, goat—each ingredient was listed with the date, quantity purchased, and the total price down to the penny. I found it a total mystery how she knew how much to buy to feed that many children.

The market was about 5 miles away, near Cité Soleil. It stretched for blocks. After we parked, Nennenn took my hand and led me into the congested jumble of stalls squeezed next to each other as far as my eyes could see. I held on tight, feeling out of place and uneasy walking into what seemed an endless maze of people and produce. Women with baskets on their heads walked about looking for customers. Others sat in stalls displaying vegetables and fruit—cabbage, carrots, onions, yams, eggplant, mangoes, pineapple, plantains, bananas—all grown by peasants in the countryside. They were stacked in piles on the ground. Some piles were fresh: a few piles were spoiling in the heat. There was no electricity or refrigeration. Seeing that food go to waste, with Cité Soleil right next door, made my heart sink.

Nennenn told me that many of the vendors slept in their stalls at night. It wasn't safe to leave their produce unattended, and it was also too far to go back and forth to their homes in the countryside. The stalls were made of cardboard and corrugated metal, or wooden poles with cloth for a roof. A rat skirted past my toes, and I jumped back, stepping on the toes of the young woman behind me. I couldn't imagine what it would be like to live and work at the market day and night. I already felt claustrophobic, and we'd been here five minutes.

Nennenn knew the market intimately and had her favorite places to shop. The first stall we went to was run by a mother and teenage daughter. They'd been expecting Nennenn and had huge bags of rice and beans set aside for her. Mother and daughter greeted us with a kiss on the cheek and motioned for me to sit down and relax on one of the rice sacks, under their cloth roof. Nennenn told me to stay there while she and Toto went deeper into the market to buy vegetables. I was nervous when she left, not wanting to let go of her hand and wishing I spoke Creole, but the smiles and gentle manner of my two guardians put me at ease.

I watched the activity of the market from my rice sack. It was packed and loud with hundreds of people shopping, selling, and bartering. I was surprised to see that the rice sacks that surrounded me in the stall had "U.S.A." stamped on them. I assumed we'd be buying Haitian-grown rice for the food program. Later, when I asked why it was U.S. rice, Fr. Gerry told me that there wasn't much rice production in Haiti anymore. In the 1980s, international lending agencies began requiring that in order to receive loans, Haiti had to reduce tariff protections for its own rice and other agricultural products, opening up the country's markets to competition from outside countries. This led to the importing of heavily subsidized U.S. rice, which was cheaper than Haitian rice. After a few years, Haiti's peasant farmers could not compete and most went out of business.

More and more farmers and agricultural workers were leaving the countryside for the city in search of employment. But most never found any. The sprawl of Cité Soleil was a reminder of the life many faced in Port-au-Prince. Those who remained in the countryside struggled to eke out a living on tiny plots of land, the soil becoming more and more depleted and water hard to find. Feeding their families and then having extra produce to sell at the market was becoming harder every year.

Still, I saw a glimmer of hope at the market. When Paul and I had flown over the parched countryside a couple of days earlier, it looked impossible to grow anything. Even Nennenn's little garden next to her house had dried up in the summer heat. But the eggplants here were a gorgeous purple, the avocados were gigantic, the oranges looked succulent. There were still some areas that had fertile soil and enough rain to produce these beautiful crops.

We loaded sacks filled with carrots, green beans, peppers, and onions into the back of the jeep. Nennenn had also bought thyme and rosemary and a few other herbs I didn't recognize. As we were about to pull out, a woman carrying a basket of garlic on her head walked by. Nennenn stopped her and they negotiated a price. Two dozen heads of garlic were added to one of our sacks. When Nennenn handed the vendor the coins and thanked her, the young woman's face lit up with excitement as she proudly put the coins in her skirt pocket and the basket back on her head.

Watching her walk gracefully down the dusty street, looking for her next customer, I thought of my friends who had trusted me with their $10, $20, or $50 bills for the food program. Now I'd seen where the money goes—to these hardworking farmers. To that woman. Not only would children at St. Clare's be fed tomorrow, but a few farmers' families would have food for the week as well.

Time to Share

As we drove into Manmi Dèt's driveway, we were greeted by the beautiful sound of children singing. Four boys from the neighborhood were belting out a church hymn as they raked the yard. A windstorm had blown through the night before, and Manmi Dèt's property was covered with broken branches and leaves. She was singing, too, supervising with her smile and enthusiasm. The kids clearly loved her and were eager to help in any way they could. When they saw us pull up, they dropped their rakes to help unload.

Two by two, the boys carried the heavy sacks to a spot under an awning adjacent to Manmi Dèt's house. This was where the cooking took place. Manmi Dèt had a large stovetop with two gas burners that could support the huge pots needed for the rice and stew. The stove was positioned under the awning, shaded from the sun, against the side of the house. Next to it on the ground was an old, blue vinyl seat from the back of a car, ripped, with the foam coming out, that served as a couch. It looked like a comfortable place to sit for the huge task of preparing the vegetables.

The boys poured a sack of carrots onto the concrete floor, got knives from Manmi Dèt, sat on cement blocks, and began peeling. They motioned for me to sit on the couch. Using the dull peeler Manmi Dèt gave me, I settled in. We were surrounded by sacks of produce, and I realized even more what an enormous task it was to prepare a meal for 500.

Manmi Dèt sat next to me with a pile of green beans and started breaking off the ends. She chatted with the boys, who ranged in age from 8 to 13. They laughed and sang more songs as they worked through the piles. Through her limited English and my limited French, I learned that these altar boys from St. Clare's Church visited almost every day. She helped them with their homework, as an old chalkboard, covered with math problems and spelling exercises, revealed. The boys were thin and dressed in tattered clothes. I was sure they were among the children who would be eating tomorrow. When Manmi Dèt brought out rice and beans for lunch, they devoured it with delight.

As the afternoon went on, our circle grew. Chef, a tall, shy man in his 70s, whose pants and shirt looked three sizes too big, pulled up a chair and started in on the eggplants. He wore a straw hat with fringed edges. Daphné, Manmi Dèt's 9-year-old granddaughter, squeezed in next to me and helped with the green beans. Nancy stopped by for a while to chop onions. A friend of Manmi Dèt's came by for a visit and ended up staying for an hour to help. Nennenn, pounding herbs in the kitchen with a mortar and pestle, checked in from time to time to see how things were going.

Preparing Sunday's meal was a community project. How rare it would be for young and old to gather like this at home. Spending an afternoon preparing a meal, singing songs, sharing jokes with family, friends, and neighbors—my life was too busy for this. Here, everyone seemed to have time, lots of time, to share.

Haitian Jezi

Manmi Dèt led Paul and me down the center aisle to a pew right in front of the lectern for the 6:30 Sunday morning Mass. The sun was inching up over the mountains, casting a soft golden hue on the sanctuary. This was one of the first times Paul and I had been together since we arrived. Ever since Fr. Gerry gave him his assignment, he'd practically lived at St. Clare's. Berry Philippe picked him up early in the morning and walked him home after dark. Paul told me he was nearly finished with the painting and felt good about it, although he was nervous about how it would be received by the congregation.

As we slipped into our seats, I glanced over my shoulder at the balcony wall. My breathing stopped for a moment while I took in the painting. It was magnificent! Jesus' almond-shaped black eyes looked right at me. His face drew me in so that I felt as if I was the only one in the room. His expression was loving and compassionate, yet strong. His outstretched arms sent chills through my body. It was as though he was inviting me to come rest in them for comfort.

My mind flashed back to the miserable nights after Rich died. Some of my most comforting moments came when I visualized being held in Jesus' arms. Each night after Luke fell asleep, I'd put on my favorite CD—Russian monks chanting—and let their deep voices sweep me away. Lying down on the carpet, I would close my eyes and picture a tranquil beach. Jesus was on it, talking to a crowd on the shoreline. Sensing my presence, he would look up and smile. The crowd would disappear, and he'd hold out his arms. I'd run through the sand, sobbing. Then he'd scoop me up like a child and carry me to the waterfront, point to the horizon, and gesture that everything would be okay.

Just the thought that Jesus was with me and that there was a divine plan of some sort helped me heal. My favorite part of the Russian chanting lasted just three minutes. When it ended, I'd press Rewind and imagine the beach scene all over again. I did this for hours.

Jesus' teachings about love and compassion, food for the hungry, and justice for those who suffer at the hands of greed and power had always been the teachings that inspired me. Maybe this is why Fr. Gerry wanted a risen Christ on the back wall. It was the last image the congregation would see before they walked back into their lives—filled with the challenges of finding clean water, feeding and clothing their families, sending children to school, and getting medicine when they were sick. Perhaps the painting would offer hope that one day their suffering might come to an end. I know Fr. Gerry's goal was to do everything he could to improve conditions in the neighborhood so that this would happen. "Let's start heaven on earth," I often heard him say.

When I turned back around in the pew, I squeezed Paul's arm with encouragement. I couldn't believe what he'd done in only two days. The Jesus he'd painted felt real and alive. I was sure the congregation would love it. While we waited for Fr. Gerry to start Mass, I reflected on the red slash Paul had painted on Jesus' ribs and the wounds in his hands. I thought about the difficult lives of the members of St. Clare's and hoped Jesus' image on the balcony wall would remind them that they were not alone in their suffering.

Beaming as usual, Fr. Gerry walked out from behind the altar to begin Mass. He looked up at the balcony and smiled. In Creole he welcomed the congregation. A couple of minutes later, when he pointed to Paul, we realized he was talking about the painting. Paul and I held our breath, knowing the moment of truth was only seconds away. With a big swoosh of his arm, Fr. Gerry dramatically pointed to the back wall and everyone turned to look. There was a gasp. Then silence. Then thunderous applause and cheers. We exhaled with relief.

After the service, congregation members stood in line to shake Paul's hand in gratitude. They gathered in the aisle in small groups, pointing and discussing the painting.

Paul brought me up to the balcony and showed me what was left of the tiny paintbrush I'd given him. It was in two pieces—the hairs of the brush had separated from the handle. He showed me the tubes of paint. The white, black, and green tubes were squeezed and rolled tight. Every drop had been used. He didn't need yellow after all. There'd been no mistakes. As we looked at the massive painting, Paul said it had nearly painted itself. We both knew it was a miracle.

As we got ready to leave the sanctuary, a middle-aged woman walked up to Paul, kissed him on the cheek, motioned to the painting, and whispered with a smile, "Haitian *Jezi.*"

The Best Day of the Week

Cooking was in full swing by the time Mass ended. A huge pot of vegetable stew was boiling on the gas stove under the awning. Two more pots of beans simmered over campfires made with sticks gathered from the yard. A teenage boy had been watching the beans cook since 3 A.M. He came each week to light the fire and get the beans started so they'd be ready on time.

Chef was back, helping chop the chicken into small pieces. He leaned on his machete, nodded hello, and wiped his forehead. The heat from the fires made it feel like 100 degrees under the awning. A woman I didn't recognize took each piece of chopped chicken and washed it in a bucket of water. Then she handed it to Nancy, who was sitting next to her on a cement block. Nancy rubbed fresh lime on both sides—to enhance the flavor, she told me. Nennenn fried the limed chicken on the stove. All the while, Manmi Dèt was scooping handfuls of rice from the 50-pound bag onto a metal plate. Gently shaking the plate, she uncovered tiny black bugs and picked them out one by one.

Nennenn waved to me to come stir the stew on the stove.

"Ah, that's good!" she declared, taking a little taste. "But we need more garlic. Garlic is good for health, Margo."

Nennenn's love for cooking showed through her smile and focus. With her wooden spoon and open heart, she moved confidently from pot to pot, adding herbs and spices.

She took her job as chef seriously and worked hard to make sure as many nutrients as possible were in each meal. For many of the children, this would be their only nutritious meal of the week. When I asked her about it, Nennenn seemed undaunted by the fact that she was making food for hundreds. She told me she never knew exactly how many children would come. Sometimes there were only 350. Sometimes 600. Usually, there was just enough food.

By 10 A.M., all that was left to do was wait for the rice to finish cooking. Daphné brought Manmi Dèt and me a cup of rich Haitian coffee, and we sipped it together on the blue vinyl couch. Manmi Dèt took my hand and squeezed it. Then she placed her other hand over her heart. Our language barrier had been frustrating. I had so many things I wanted to ask and tell her. But her beautiful gestures spoke volumes.

I decided to try my French, and I asked her what she thought of the food program. She understood my question and replied—part in English, part in French.

"It's good . . . *parce que les enfants ont faim*" (because the children are hungry).

She paused and took a sip of coffee.

"I like . . . because I love the poor . . . *Je veux imiter Jésus*" (I want to imitate Jesus). She pointed in the direction of the pink church on the hill. *"Sainte Claire imite Jésus."*

I nodded in agreement, feeling the sincerity of her words.

We sat in silence, watching Nennenn stir the stew and then dish up two plates. She proudly handed us each a generous portion. "Eat. Eat." Her eyes sparkled as she watched me take a bite and chew it slowly. I could taste a hint of lime in my chicken. The tender vegetables were blended in a delicious sauce. It wasn't spicy, just alive with flavor.

"I love it!" I exclaimed, to Nennenn's delight.

She slapped her leg and laughed. "Good. That's good!"

Chef and the other volunteers lined up eagerly at the stove with empty containers they'd brought. Nennenn filled each one up to the top with rice, beans, stew, and chicken. I realized then that they were taking meals home to their families.

The pots were hauled into the back of Toto's jeep, and we left for the church rectory. Along the way, I spotted dozens of children walking from all directions, on their way to the meal site.

I remembered Father Gerry's e-mail description of Sundays in this neighborhood. "You should hear what they say about the hot meal they receive on Sundays. They say that Sunday is the best day of the week. They cannot wait to have Sunday. Sunday is too far away sometimes for those who are hungry."

Manje!

When we pulled up to the rectory, yet another batch of volunteers greeted us. They wore the neatly pressed red-and-white-striped aprons that Manmi Dèt had made on her foot-pedal sewing machine. They'd been busy washing floors, arranging wooden tables and benches, stacking clean bowls and spoons, and placing plastic tablecloths on the tables. The table coverings reminded me of the thin, cheap ones I bought for Luke's birthday parties only to throw away after one use. I could tell these had been used over and over, treated with the kind of care given a silk or lace tablecloth.

The rectory was larger than I'd imagined. It was a two-story white stone building—about 2,000 square feet—surrounded by an acre of dirt and rock. The first floor was empty, except for the wooden tables and benches that had been brought in for the food program. A stairway led to the second floor, which was home to three young men who helped out at St. Clare's. We moved the pots of food into the rectory's back room. I spotted a sink and counter, but no plumbing.

Within minutes of our arrival, a long line of children formed outside the front door, ranging in age from 2 to late teens. I wondered how far some of them had walked and when their last meal had been. Some looked weak and tired. Others were jumping up and down with excitement. Many wore their Sunday best—girls in bridesmaid dresses or lacy Easter dresses with big bows—probably hand-me-downs from the States. Their brightly colored hair ribbons matched their outfits and blew in the breeze. Most of the boys wore white dress shirts or T-shirts and faded pants that had been passed down brother to brother. Their belts were pulled to the last notch. Many of the children's shoes had broken straps, no laces, and were either too big or too small. But even with clothes that didn't fit, they wore them with a dignity I'd noticed over and over in Haiti.

Watching this massive event unfold, I shook my head and laughed as I thought of all the church committee meetings I'd sat through where it seemed to take months, if not years, to get a new project started. Finding volunteers always seemed a monumental challenge. Not here. The community of St. Clare's had their meal program for 500 up and running within a couple of weeks after receiving the first funding check.

Everyone moved quickly to get the youngest children seated on benches in the two front rooms of the rectory. The meal would be served in shifts, since there was room for only about 150 to eat at one time. A circle of women sat on cement blocks in the back room and started to dish up plates. They sang and talked as they worked. One put a scoop of steaming rice on the plate and passed it to her right, where beans and a piece of chicken were added. Then the plate was passed again and a generous helping of stew was poured over the top, filling it to overflowing. The delicious aroma flowed through the open windows and doors. You could feel the anticipation rise outside as the children waited to be served.

Twenty more volunteers, most of them children, lined up shoulder to shoulder to form a human chain that extended all the way from the circle of women to the tables in the front of the rectory. They were proudly dressed in their aprons and passed the plates of hot food slowly and carefully from one to the next. I was sure they were as hungry as the children at the tables, and there were definitely more than enough volunteers, but they wanted to help. With smiles and concentration they took their task seriously—keeping the plates flowing. I spotted Berry Philippe and the four boys who had helped peel carrots standing in the middle of the chain.

When the food was placed in front of the children, I was amazed that they didn't eat right away. Even 2- and 3-year-olds sat patiently with their hands at their sides waiting until everyone was served. Then, a woman I recognized from church that morning clapped her hands to get the children's attention. She lifted her arms and directed them in a song of thanksgiving. They all knew it well and sang enthusiastically. Their voices filled the rectory and were probably heard blocks away. The song ended with everyone clapping and singing, *"Mèsi, Bondye, mèsi!"* (Thank you, God.) *"Amen. Amen. Amen."*

The time they'd been waiting for had arrived. I studied their faces as they spooned in Nennenn's stew. They were focused—chewing and swallowing with urgency and excitement. Famished. Their eyes were serious, but many of them still had a sparkle. I watched the littlest ones keep up with their older siblings, completing gigantic portions in record time. They scraped their plates clean with their spoons and then ran their tongues over them, licking every drop. I thought of the mother of three from Son Fils and the days we spent together. I wondered if she was still alive, and if her children knew about the food program.

Plates passing, spoons scraping, people singing, children laughing—the scene was festive, like a party. When the first shift of children finished eating, they cleared and washed their plates and another 150 children filed into the rectory.

Father Gerry arrived as the meal was coming to a close. I could hear his laugh over all the excitement. He sat on a bench next to the children and invited me to join him. Helping himself to a plate of stew, he said, "You see, Margaret, we have the feeling of great sharing at this food program. Share, share, share: that produces love, love, love. Love for God and love for everyone. We love each other and we love all of you who are helping us help ourselves."

"Manje?" a child asked.

"Non, mèsi," I said as I looked at the growing crowd of adults waiting close by in eager anticipation of the leftovers they hoped would be served to them. The volunteers were eating now. Berry Philippe sat down next to Fr. Gerry and me, looked up, and smiled with relief and satisfaction as he dug into his meal. Paul told me Berry's father had died a few years before and that his mother was very ill. He had eight brothers and sisters and no source of income. When Paul asked Berry whether he'd eaten the day he'd helped find the chalk, Berry had said yes—he'd had a small piece of bread and a packet of sugar.

As I helped wash dishes and put away pots and pans, I noticed a mother wearing a sun-faded red dress. She was slowly walking out of the rectory with her two young children. I hoped there had been an extra plate for her. She looked weak and tired, as though she was about to collapse. She reminded me of the women at Son Fils. Her face was gaunt and serious as she lovingly held the hands of her children and made her way into the dusty street and disappeared around the corner. Other children filed out of the yard behind her. They looked happy and full, but what did the rest of the week hold for them? I guessed it would be only a few hours before they all felt hungry again.

Piti Piti Na Rive

On our last day, just before we left for the airport, Fr. Gerry took me on a drive around the neighborhood while Paul stayed behind at St. Clare's to use every minute to touch up his Jesus painting. As Fr. Gerry and I drove through the narrow streets of the St. Clare's community, he called out *"Bonjou"* to everyone he passed. A naked 3-year-old boy tore out of his house, jumped up and down, and squealed with excitement when he heard Fr. Gerry's voice.

"Okay, okay," Fr. Gerry laughed, pulling over and reaching for the plastic container of jellybeans he kept on the front seat. Within seconds, a dozen giggling kids swarmed his window, hands outstretched. He placed a jellybean in each palm. *"Mèsi! Mèsi!"* they said as they cradled their treat. I watched them lick and carefully chew their jellybean, and I thought of Luke's annual pillowcase filled with Halloween candy, his overflowing Christmas stocking, Easter basket, and the more-than-occasional treats I bought him at the store. Here, one jellybean was precious!

We had started to pull away when a young mother ran up to the jeep holding a piece of paper that had a scrap of green-and-white-checkered cloth pinned to it. That was the fabric needed for a school uniform. She fought back tears as she whispered something to Fr. Gerry, who listened patiently, then reassured her. Looking relieved, she walked away.

I asked what was wrong, and he explained that she couldn't afford to send her daughter to school. Only 10 percent of schools in Haiti are public. Even though President Aristide and President Préval had built over 300 new public schools during their terms, all of them were full. The alternative, private school, costs $100 U.S. per year or more, well beyond the means of this mother and most Haitians.

"Can you help her?" I asked.

"I'm going to try," he said.

I sat back and stared out the window. How could he be so hopeful in the midst of such overwhelming poverty? I couldn't forget the face of the mother in the faded red dress at the food program. Her sunken cheekbones and fragility made me think she didn't have many days left to live. The excitement of watching the children eat faded for me as soon as they left the rectory. The reality of their lives, the daily hunger, filled me with sadness. Yet, Fr. Gerry didn't seem tired or weighed down by the struggles of his community.

"Margaret, I have something to show you," he said as we pulled into the driveway of the rectory, a short way down the hill from St. Clare's Church. The building was quiet, an empty shell compared to the day before. It was rarely used during the week, although Fr. Gerry had big plans. We walked across the dusty yard to the right side of the building.

"This is where the outdoor cafeteria will be. A large space for the food program to be served. Three hundred children will be able to sit down at once." His eyes smiled and his voice was convincing.

"An outdoor cafeteria?" I said, confused.

He nodded. "With a roof and sturdy tables and benches for the children, and a concrete floor so they won't hurt themselves on the rocks and glass." He led me around the corner and pointed to the back of the rectory building. "Right here is where the new kitchen will go. With running water and a big stove to cook food, so we can serve meals to the children all week long."

I squinted in the sunlight, trying to imagine the new kitchen and the possibility of more days of food.

With a big smile, he continued, "Over here is where the school will go." He pointed to the empty half-acre lot on the left side of the rectory. "With a daily lunch, a library, and a health clinic. And over there"—he spun around and pointed to the road leading to the rectory—"I see the roads paved. No more roads that wash away each time it rains. No more struggling to get up the hill." Then he turned slowly in a circle, pointing to the homes surrounding us. "Margaret, I see all the children fed and their parents working. Everyone has enough food to eat and electricity and running water."

I looked with him into the neighborhood, past the piles of garbage and the dark interiors of the dilapidated homes, trying to imagine his vision. But I couldn't. The bleak reality overwhelmed me. So I shut my eyes and tilted my head back. The sun burned my cheeks as I tried to picture a school next to the rectory. After a few seconds, it began to take shape. It was three stories high—bright blue, orange, and yellow. Happy colors. I imagined a bell ringing and dozens of children skipping through the gate, books in their arms, chatting and laughing as they walked into classrooms and sat behind new desks, their teachers greeting them.

"Father Gerry?" I opened my eyes quickly, excited about this vision. "Do you think I should start exploring grants to raise money for the school? How much do you think it will cost?"

He laughed, "First Margaret, we feed the children, we keep them alive. Then the school."

Fr. Gerry glanced at his watch. It was time to pick up Paul and drive to the airport. As we walked through the yard and back to the jeep, Fr. Gerry turned to me and said, "We have a Creole saying I want to teach you. *'Piti piti na rive.'* That means little by little we will arrive. One step at a time, Margaret. In Haiti, sometimes they are very, very small steps." He laughed another of his full belly laughs. "Sometimes we go backward. But it's important to keep taking steps, even though they are small. Never lose hope. Never give up. One day, maybe not during my lifetime, but one day, we will get there."

PART III

*They nourished
and fed my soul*

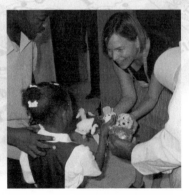

Kado!

Eight weeks later I was back in the crowded airport in Port-au-Prince. It was my third visit to Haiti. This time, I had Luke with me, and four 75-pound duffel bags stuffed with toys for the children.

Luke and I had made a collection before leaving, asking the first- through sixth-graders at his school to donate "like new" Beanie Babies, SuperBalls, Hot Wheels cars, and other small gifts. No need to shop, I told them. If Luke's room was any indication, they had plenty of beautiful, unplayed-with toys in their own bedrooms to share. I was right. Toys filled my living room the night before we left. Luke and I counted each one to be sure we had enough—900! Just about enough for each child to receive two.

We'd planned this visit to Haiti quickly. I had a business conference in Miami and decided that it was too close to St. Clare's not to go. There were so many things I wanted to learn more about—education, health care, drinking water—that any opportunity to visit Port-au-Prince, even for only three days, felt important. So I e-mailed Fr. Gerry and bought two tickets. Just nine months earlier, when I went to Haiti for the first time, the process of flying to Port-au-Prince was huge, logistically and emotionally. Now it was starting to feel normal—almost like visiting another state. We arrived on a Sunday morning, just in time for the food program.

Since Fr. Gerry was leading Mass, he told us to look for a "Margaret Trost" sign when we landed. The man carrying it would drive us to St. Clare's. But as I looked around the airport, I didn't see him anywhere. We sat on our luggage and waited. Five minutes. Ten. Twenty. I wasn't sure what to do.

Should we just stay put? I didn't want to miss the food program. I'm usually so thorough and organized, but I'd forgotten to ask for the phone number at St. Clare's. I didn't even know the address.

"Taxi?" A man in a baggy navy blue suit approached and pointed to the door. His smile and gentle manner seemed trustworthy.

"*Oui,*" I said hesitantly, wondering whether climbing in the backseat of his battered white taxi was safe.

"*Addresse?*"

I described St. Clare's Church, hoping he'd heard of it—up on a hill, peach-colored, close to the airport, Fr. Gerry. His face was blank. Whistling to a couple of porters, he consulted with them for directions. Nobody seemed to know where it was. They called over more porters, and finally the huddle of men agreed we should go straight, then left, then right.

As we inched along in traffic, the driver peered down street after street, unsure where to turn. I began to think I should have stayed at the airport. I clutched Luke and my backpack and studied the streets, trying to recognize something from my last visit with Paul—the corner soda store, the kindergarten school near Manmi Dèt's house. I didn't have her address either. Her neighborhood didn't have street signs or numbers on the houses. All the streets we passed looked the same—vendors and shacks and barefoot children walking around selling gum or hoping to wash car windshields for a penny.

Twisting and turning through the maze of streets, we eventually came to an empty dirt soccer field. It looked familiar, like one I remembered seeing near the rectory. I started to get excited as I studied the houses. The more I looked at them, the more familiar they seemed. "Over there," I guessed. We turned right, proceeded down a narrow road, turned right again, and sure enough, there was the white two-story church rectory. St. Clare's was just a few hundred yards up the hill. I could hear the congregation singing.

The children were already gathering at the rectory for the noon meal. "Luke, we're here!" I didn't even want to think of what could have happened, only that we'd made it safely. *"Mèsi, mèsi!"* I jumped out of the backseat and shook our driver's hand.

He flashed a smile. *"Pa gen pwoblèm"* (No problem), he said as he unloaded our bags.

Nennenn heard the taxi and ran to greet us. She pinched Luke's cheeks and kissed his forehead over and over. When she unzipped the green duffel bags, she gasped at the sight of the hundreds of toys. *"Kado!"* She pulled out a doll and squeezed it. "The children are going to be so happy!"

The kitchen was hopping with activity. Plates were already being dished up. The line of children grew quickly as they waited for the door to open. Standing on tiptoe, they tried to peek through the door's metal grate to see what was going on inside. They could smell Nennenn's creation.

Nennenn gave the word, and the door flung open. Hundreds of kids filed in. The girls went upstairs, the boys stayed on the main floor. They'd expanded to the second floor, putting tables and benches for another 100 in an open-air porch area. The children slid next to each other on the benches, filling the tables in a matter of seconds. Immediately, plates started to flow out of the kitchen. Nennenn liked the meal served hot. The human chain of volunteers went up the stairs and into two rooms on the main floor. *"Mèsi, Bondye, mèsi!"* (Thank you, God.) From upstairs the girls' enthusiastic voices singing grace filled the rectory. Soon the boys seated downstairs started singing their prayer. Then, after a nod from an adult in each room, all I could hear for several minutes was the sound of spoons scraping plates.

Luke and I stayed in the kitchen to help the servers. Luke's face was serious as he watched the children eating, through a window. Many of them were his age. As much as I'd talked about the hunger in Haiti, it hadn't been real to him until that moment.

By the time Fr. Gerry arrived, most of the children had finished eating. He was so relieved to see us. He said his assistant was still looking for us at the airport and was worried something had happened. I told him about the nice taxi driver and then showed him the bags stuffed with toys. He gave us a hug and turned to make an announcement to the children. Although I could not understand exactly what he said, I recognized the word *kado*, which means "present."

The room lit up with screams of excitement. Hands clapped, bodies squirmed. Nennenn proudly opened the first duffel bag and Beanie Babies made their way down the bench and up the stairs. So did Hot Wheels cars, yoyos, SuperBalls, dolls. Luke asked Nennenn if he could help her pass out the toys. Within minutes, the rectory looked like a carnival. Laughter, games, children playing everywhere. Some huddled in a corner with their Beanie Babies. Others raced tiny cars through the gravel outside. Older girls braided their new dolls' hair. SuperBalls flew around. Chaos. Joy. Tears. Luke was in the middle of it all, surrounded by kids, handing out the gifts from his classmates. I caught a glimpse of him, overwhelmed by the crowd, holding toys over his head and trying to pass them out one at a time.

I sat down on the bench to watch the children play. The kitchen servers were eating now, looking on with big smiles. Next to me was a 5-year-old boy, quietly holding the little red fire engine he'd received. He slowly moved it back and forth on the table top, watching the wheels turn. He moved his fingers over the red paint, studying the engine's shape. I watched him hold his new toy as if it was the most precious thing he owned. I thought of all the children at Luke's school who had gone through their overstuffed closets and shelves to select toys to share. I didn't think they had any idea what joy just one toy would give a child.

Luke joined me on the bench. He was happy and exhausted. I put my arm around him, and he rested his head on my shoulder. I was so glad I'd brought him with me. Since my first trip to Haiti, we'd had several conversations about how much more we have than most people in the world and how important it is to share. I knew this was a day my 8-year-old would never forget—a day when he'd experienced sharing on a grand scale and the joy it brings both the giver and the receiver.

Students

A bulb dangled from a wire high in the middle of the ceiling, but there wasn't any light to brighten the tiny classroom. The electricity was off again that day. The children, 8 to 14 years old, were dressed in blue-and-white-checked uniforms, sitting shoulder to shoulder on the four rows of wooden benches, their knees touching the backs of the child in front of them. I counted fifty. When I walked in to greet them, they rose politely and said in unison, *"Bonjour, mademoiselle. Bonjour, mon père."* Fr. Gerry was with me. It was Monday morning.

I'd asked Fr. Gerry to take me to a school in the St. Clare's neighborhood, so I could see where we might be able to enroll children from the food program if I could raise tuition money. I remembered the mother with the piece of green-and-white-checkered cloth who had come up to Fr. Gerry's jeep a couple of months earlier. My hope was that if there was money left over after we paid for the food program, we could start sending children to school—one at a time. *Piti piti,* Little by little.

The teacher, a young man with a bright smile, enthusiastically wrote third-grade math problems on the blackboard as the students concentrated on the lesson. Thankfully there was a small window that let in a little light and some fresh air. But other than the window and the chalkboard, benches, a few pieces of paper and pencils, and a handful of books, there wasn't much more to the classroom. The walls were unpainted cement blocks. The window didn't have a screen or curtains. I searched for science projects, art supplies, posters, a globe. Nothing. Luke's personal back-to-school supply list had more items on it than what was in that entire classroom.

But the room was anything but dead. The students were focused and serious. I wondered how it was possible for them to sit so close to each other without teasing or fighting or goofing off. But that didn't seem to be a problem. No one fidgeted. No one spoke out of turn. No one stared out the window. I didn't think it was a performance for me. I felt their eagerness to learn. These kids wanted to be there.

As I leaned against the classroom wall and watched the children concentrate on the blackboard, I noticed some of them squinting. Maybe it was the dim light, but maybe they needed glasses. It occurred to me that I'd never seen a Haitian child wearing glasses. A well-used Pokémon backpack peeked out from under one child's legs. It looked empty, but I hoped there was a lunch in it. I wondered how many of these children ate breakfast and whether they'd have homework that night. Did they have pencil sharpeners in case their pencil tip broke? Paper to write on? Did they do their homework by candlelight? Some of the children were so much older than the others. I wondered how they felt being in a class with children much younger than they were.

"Un, deux, trois, quatre." The enthusiastic voices of first-grade students in another classroom distracted my thoughts. They were learning to count in French. Only 15 percent of Haitians speak French, yet the education system has always been conducted in French. Every child needs to become fluent in order to understand the lessons. Historically, this has been a way to separate the "elite" Haitians, who speak primarily French, from the poor majority, who speak Creole. Although Creole was being spoken more in schools since President Aristide's first term, French was still the primary language of education. Most land titles were written in French. The justice system and all government business were conducted primarily in French. Having to learn another language in order to read and write, and the lack of free education and adult literacy programs, were reasons why Haiti's illiteracy rate was so high—50 percent.

The voices of the students learning to count didn't disturb the kids I was with. The math lesson continued. I looked to see if there was a door that could be shut but realized it was broken, allowing the sounds of learning to float freely from one space to the next.

As I walked out of the school, a little girl about 8 or 9 crossed the street in front of us. She was wearing torn pink sneakers and carried two large pails of water. She set down her load and looked up at the window, where she could hear the lesson being taught. Her face revealed how much she wished she could be learning, too, but carrying water was her job that day and probably every day. She picked up her buckets and continued down the dusty road.

La Maison des Enfants

I walked tentatively up to the blue gate and peeked in. I was nervous about volunteering at La Maison des Enfants, a home for orphans and children who were critically ill. But I had nothing planned for the morning and Manmi Dèt was happy to watch Luke. Like Son Fils, the facility was run by the Missionaries of Charity and was the last hope for families with sick children who couldn't afford to pay a doctor. It was the only hope for the dozens of orphans who lived there.

I lifted the latch, went in, and was greeted by a nun wearing a light-blue sari and habit. Fr. Gerry had arranged my visit. My mentioning his name brought a big smile to her face as she escorted me into the two-story building.

"The sick children are in the room to the right. The others are through that door straight ahead. There's a play yard in the back. Please go wherever you'd like."

As I stood in the middle of the room debating where to go, six children burst through the door. They hugged my knees and pulled me over to a straw stool. Before I knew it, three of them were in my lap. They were so tiny and light, there was actually room for them. One played with my hair, fascinated with its golden color and straightness. Another rested his head on my shoulder. A little girl stroked my cheek, turning my head to face hers every time I looked away. They were maybe 4 or 5 years old. The others anxiously waited their turn. I sensed their fear that I would leave before they got their chance to be close, so I let them hold a finger and drew them into the huddle. A few minutes later, bowls of creamy rice were passed out. The children on my lap ran to their eating spots, waving as they left.

With six rooms filled with beds on the first floor and more on the second, I guessed that about seventy or eighty children

lived there. Most of them were 10 or younger. About twenty
babies and toddlers were in the front rooms, the area for sick
children. I decided to stay with them. Looking into each of
their cribs, I could see that many were close to death. Their
bodies were emaciated, their breathing shallow, their eyes
withdrawn. They didn't have any interest in the plastic play
boards strapped to their crib railing. Occasionally one would
cry. But for the number of babies in the room, it was ominously quiet. I saw two IVs, but no other evidence of intensive care equipment. I glanced into the nun's supply room
and saw a handful of medicines on the shelf, and the books
Tropical Medicine and *Where There Is No Doctor.*

I watched in awe as the nuns patiently changed tiny cloth
diapers, wiped away tears, and spoon-fed breakfast. They
were always busy with a task—not hurried or stressed, but
continually moving. The work it took to meet the needs of
all these children—how did they do it? I was emotionally exhausted after just one hour, and started glancing at the clock
to count the minutes until Fr. Gerry would pick me up. I
couldn't fathom being there every day like the nuns.

At ten o'clock, parents of the sick children arrived. Tues-
day was visiting day, and I could hear a crowd gathering outside. When the gate opened, mothers and fathers rushed to
hold their children. The scene was heartbreaking, as I wondered how many of their babies would be alive when they
returned next week.

In just a couple of minutes, all the cribs in the room had
a visitor, except for one. One baby was left, a little boy. I
walked over to him and looked down. He was tiny, too frail
to be moved, I thought, but then he reached out to me.

"May I pick him up?" I asked as a nun passed by.

"Of course." She smiled.

"How old is he?"

"Eighteen months."

Eighteen months! He didn't look older than five or six weeks. His skin wrinkled on his bones. His head wobbled like a newborn. I didn't think he weighed more than 8 pounds. As I positioned him in my arms, he snuggled close to my chin. I rocked him back and forth and hummed a lullaby. He was silent, so silent I was afraid he'd stopped breathing, but then I felt his tiny chest rise and fall so I stopped worrying. Where were his parents? Maybe his mother died giving birth to him. Maternal mortality rates were high in Haiti. So were infant mortality rates. I wondered why he was sick—maybe cholera.

As I stood in the room holding that tiny child, I wondered about all the other children in Haiti and throughout the world whose lives are cut short from malnutrition or contaminated water. The statistics are overwhelming and discouraging. And now I was holding one of those statistics. The situation was palpably real, and I felt my cheeks flush with anger at the thought that these children were dying from easily preventable and curable diseases.

When Fr. Gerry arrived at noon, I kissed the baby's gaunt cheek and laid him in the crib. I grabbed my bag and left, feeling my heart break as I watched him reach his hand out for me and cry.

I walked to the street and passed two women carrying sick babies in their arms, on their way to La Maison des Enfants in hopes there might be room for them. But every crib was full and the only way their children could be admitted was if another child recovered, or died. I ached to think that the next open crib might be the one of the little boy I'd just kissed good-bye.

Water

Manmi Dèt and I had just started climbing the hill to
St. Clare's Church for Mass. I was thrilled to be able
to go to a service before Luke and I returned to
Berkeley. Thick, black clouds were moving quickly over the
mountains and seemed to be racing us to church. We grabbed
each other's hand and dashed for the sanctuary, while vendors rushed to cover their fruit stands, and those walking in
the street ducked into the nearest shelter. Kids playing soccer with a crushed soda can stopped and took cover, too.
Within seconds, the fierce storm drenched the whole neighborhood and turned the road into a river.

A young boy, about 13, walked casually across the church-
yard, undisturbed by the wind and rain. He was carrying a
bar of soap in his hand. I watched him stop at the corner of
the church, and position himself directly under a stream of
water that poured off the pitched roof. The water rushed
down at the perfect angle for an outdoor shower. There, in
the middle of the afternoon in the midst of thunder and light-
ning, he stood in his shorts and washed his hair, face, and
body, rinsed off, and walked back home.

No one in the neighborhood had running water. Fr. Gerry
told me the water pipes broke five years earlier, and the city
couldn't afford to fix them. Instead, women and children
spent their days walking back and forth on the rugged roads
to get water from a pump.

Most of the diseases that kill Haitian children come from
drinking contaminated water. Bacteria thrive in untreated,
unfiltered water, rusty pipes, and dirty faucets. Some of the
kids I saw carrying water on the side of the road were using
old paint or oil containers as their buckets.

It's even harder to find potable water in the countryside. People climb up and down the mountainside to dip their jugs in rivers and streams. During part of the year, some of these natural water sources dry up, making the search for water even more difficult. Deforestation has turned much of Haiti into a near desert, where the rainy season is no longer predictable. No wonder Fr. Gerry said that water is the most precious, needed resource in Haiti.

The storm moved through quickly. As I sat next to Manmi Dèt in the second pew on the left, I looked at the women seated with us and wondered if they felt as thirsty as I did. They must have. Sweat poured down their faces and necks, but they sang and prayed and followed the liturgy with an attention and devotion that rose above thirst. I waited patiently for the service to end, wishing that I could stop thinking about water. But it was so hot, the humidity was thick, and the fans weren't working. Later when Manmi Dèt poured me a tall glass of bottled water in her kitchen, I thought about the little girl in pink sneakers and wondered whether the water she was carrying was safe.

The next morning, Luke and I flew home. The scenes of the gift distribution, the schoolroom, the orphanage, and the afternoon storm remained fixed in my mind. I'd only spent a few days in the Tiplas Kazo community on my trip with Paul and my trip with Luke, but I felt a growing connection to it. There was something about Fr. Gerry, the Dépestre family, the children, and everyone at St. Clare's that nourished me and fed my soul.

As I watched the Haitian coast disappear beneath my airplane window, I wondered where it all would lead. I had no idea. But uncharacteristically for me, I didn't feel the need to know at that time. I was content to accept the mystery,

PART IV

*You're here
to love*

Kenbe Fèm!

Every room in my house in Berkeley had something to remind me of Haiti. The painting from Cité Soleil hung in my bedroom. A stone carving of a woman holding a baby was on my kitchen counter. Pictures of Fr. Gerry, Manmi Dèt, Nennenn, and the children of the food program were taped to the borders of my computer screen. I thought about them all the time.

After the trip with Luke, I felt an urgency to tell people what I had experienced. Between packing lunches, driving Luke to and from school, and running my health and wellness business, I sent e-mails and made phone calls to friends, describing the school, the boy who took his shower in the rain, and the children who came to eat at the food program. I wrote about Manmi Dèt and Nennenn and their dedication to providing healthy meals every Sunday. I shared Fr. Gerry's words, *Piti piti na rive,* and his vision of hope.

I also told them I had decided to create a nonprofit corporation, with the help of an attorney friend, so I could raise the funds needed for the food program. It was clear from my visits that the members of St. Clare's were determined to keep it going, and so was I. I needed to think of a name for the nonprofit, and one day while I was praying, two words came to mind as clearly as if they'd been written on a piece of paper: What if?

Before I could wonder what this meant, a stream of "what if" questions came to me. What if every child in the Tiplas Kazo neighborhood had three meals a day? What if every child had not only enough food, but clean water, education, shelter, and health care? What if providing these necessities to children was the world's priority? What if the economic and political systems that perpetuate poverty were transformed? One "What if?" question after another entered my mind, pointing to possibilities and hope.

When I opened my eyes, I knew one thing for sure. The name. In January 2001, one year after my first visit to Haiti, the What If? Foundation was founded, and I became its volunteer director, administrator, and fund-raiser.

A friend sent an e-mail commenting on what a burden I must feel taking on the responsibility to raise the money needed to feed 500 children once a week. It was a huge commitment, she said, since whether they ate or not would depend on me. I hadn't thought about it that way before. Sharing the story of the children in Tiplas Kazo and collecting funds for the food program didn't feel like a burden. It was a fulfillment, the new purpose I'd been searching for since Rich died. It was an opportunity to help others in a very personal way, and it made me extremely happy. I didn't worry about the future or what it might mean to keep things going month after month. From the moment I met Fr. Gerry and heard his vision of a food program, I felt swept up in the flow of something beautiful. I didn't feel the need to question or worry about it. I just went with it.

As the weeks passed, checks continued to arrive in my mailbox—$50, $25, $100. A friend's daughter sent the contents of her piggy bank. Another friend sent the proceeds from a bake sale. Business associates held a raffle. My former church in Wisconsin sent $1,000 and made a commitment to support the program annually. A friend's Rotary Club sent $1,500. Friends of friends, strangers to me, sent checks too. I deposited the money in the What If? Foundation's bank account in Berkeley and then wired it to the food program's account in Haiti. Fr. Gerry withdrew what was needed and gave it to Nennenn, so she could shop at the farmers' market. Meticulous notes were kept describing how every penny was spent. Our simple system worked.

Each time I received a check, I multiplied the amount by two and wrote the donor letting them know how many meals they'd just made possible. Ten dollars fed twenty children. One hundred dollars fed 200 children. At 50 cents a meal, every check made a difference. Donors wrote that they liked the simplicity and intimacy of the program. By knowing me and hearing about my experiences, they understood the hunger of the children in a more real and personal way, and they were grateful to be able to help.

I forwarded e-mails from Fr. Gerry to keep them connected and informed.

> Dear Margaret,
>
> The food program remains a great help to the hungry ones. We may have to change the name Sun-day to Food-day. Food may be understood as both spiritual and material. Thanks a lot to you and to all the friends who freely and lovingly are helping. *Kenbe fèm!* (Hold on firm.)
>
> Gerry

> Dear Margaret,
>
> The Sunday meal is a standard program now for the needy children, teenagers, and some adults. After the church worship it is the greatest act of love for me—to help feed the hungry ones. It is tough some days, but it is a must. Jesus loves, loves, loves it. The children appreciate it so much. They come from all over. They walk miles for a hot, blessed meal served with God's love within us all.
>
> Gerry

Each time I heard from Fr. Gerry, I felt my heart longing to return to Haiti. On a spring afternoon, as I listened to an audiotape of the St. Clare's choir that Fr. Gerry had given me and stared at a picture of Manmi Dèt, I got an idea. What if Luke and I went to Haiti for the summer? Manmi Dèt had invited me to come back for as long as I wanted, and assured me it would not be an imposition. I'd never before considered going for more than a week at a time, but the thought of being in Port-au-Prince with Luke for a couple of months intrigued me. I was exhausted, both physically and emotionally, from a whirlwind pace that seemed to fill every second of every day—fund-raising, working on my business, and taking care of Luke. I felt drained, unable to find balance, and I could feel the onset of burnout. A summer in Haiti could help me rejuvenate.

The more I thought about it, the more I loved the idea. During a longer visit, I could learn some Creole and become more connected to the community, and it would be an incredible experience for Luke. But more than anything else, I just wanted to be with the members of St. Clare's. I e-mailed Fr. Gerry, who wrote back that Manmi Dèt was waiting for us. "This is your home," she said.

I started to write down what it would take for the trip to happen. As the list got longer and longer, it seemed more and more crazy. But it felt so right. I kept writing. Luke would be out of school in mid-June. Check. My sister could look after my house and mail. Check. With proper planning, my business could run on its own for a while. Check.

Family and friends were surprised when I told them my plans. They were supportive, but I could tell they were concerned for our safety. I reassured them that things were calm politically in Haiti. The majority of Haitians were very supportive of President Aristide, whom they had elected a few months earlier in a landslide victory. Although living conditions remained exceedingly difficult, there was relative security and peace throughout the country. It was a good time to visit.

I told Luke, who immediately started talking about introducing the St. Clare kids to his favorite sport—baseball. His Little League season had just begun, so he spread the word at the fields and started a collection for extra gloves, hats, jerseys, and balls. It grew every week.

The plans for spending the summer in Port-au-Prince brought a renewed sense of energy and excitement to my days. Time passed quickly, and before I knew it, Luke and I left Berkeley with a small suitcase of clothes, malaria pills, and four duffel bags packed with school supplies and baseball gear. I just knew I was doing the right thing. Everything had fallen into place.

Fruit Salad

We arrived at Manmi Dèt's from the airport just as Nennenn was returning from the farmers' market with baskets of ripe mangoes, bananas, pineapples, melons, and oranges. The family was getting ready to make a fruit salad for a special meal that was planned for priests visiting St. Clare's. The air was warm and sticky, and the summer sun beat down with intensity. I quickly changed into my lightest sundress and joined Manmi Dèt and the others under the awning. We ate fried plantains, my favorite Haitian treat. I felt right at home, as though I'd never left.

Chairs and cement blocks were arranged in a circle, with the fruit piled in the center. Manmi Dèt motioned for me to sit next to her on the blue couch with no legs. She handed me a small knife and an orange. With their loving companionship, all the gorgeous fruit, and a slight breeze waving the palm fronds overhead, it felt for a moment like I was back in the Cayman Islands, except that I'd just come from the airport and had seen the miserable living conditions for the millions who lived in Port-au-Prince.

I studied the piles of fruit and found myself calculating how long it would take to prepare all this. Fruit juice dripped down my arms and beads of sweat formed on my forehead as I whipped through my mound of oranges, peeling the skins with focus and determination. I was excited about the progress I was making.

I finally took a break to sip a bottle of Haitian cola Manmi Dèt had given me, and looked around. It was obvious the Dépestre women and I did not share the same rhythm. They'd hardly made a dent in their sides of the pile. They laughed and joked and talked and teased. Slowly and carefully they cut each mango and melon into the tiniest pieces I'd ever seen. I couldn't help but wonder why they were cutting them so small. At this pace, we'd be here all afternoon.

And then I remembered—that was the point. I remembered the *poudre d'amour* dessert that was served in 500 plastic bags. I remembered the reason I'd come to Haiti. There was no need to rush or to multitask. I took a deep breath and started again, this time trying to cut my oranges as delicately as Manmi Dèt cut her mangoes.

But I couldn't do it. My hands just sped up, as if in a race. I was locked into a different speed, and realized it might take the whole two months just to stop my compulsion to check things off a list and find ways to do more things in less time. I was an expert at folding laundry while making business calls—with a headset so both hands were free—and monitoring dinner on the stove at the same time. I was always in a hurry, trying to get as much done as possible before Luke got home from school. But now I was in Haiti. I didn't have a day planner or a list of to-dos or any major responsibilities.

I put down my orange, took another sip of cola, and observed my friends. Very delicately, with extremely dull knives, they cut into the succulent fruit and really seemed to enjoy it. Every seed was removed, every extraneous piece of pulp pulled out.

Manmi Dèt was in charge of mangoes. She positioned each one in a way that made it easy to run the knife down each side of the pit, separating the pit from the fruit. Then she held up a section and carved lines in it from top to bottom and then side to side, like tic-tac-toe. When she bent the mango skin back, the chunks of fruit popped right up. Then she cut along the skin, and the tiny squares fell right into the bowl. She made it look so easy.

I watched Magga, Manmi Dèt's daughter-in-law, work on cutting pineapples. Instead of adding her tiny chunks to the bowl that held my cut oranges and Manmi Dèt's mango, she poured all her hard work into a strainer and mashed it into juice. So much effort to make those tiny pieces, only to turn them into juice. With a wooden spoon, she gently pressed the pineapple against the strainer in a circular motion until the sweet drops squeezed out of the tiny mesh and onto the growing mound of fruit salad. When she was done, she scraped the pulp out of the strainer and into another bowl. Nothing was ever wasted. I was sure it would be eaten later.

Luke slipped in between Manmi Dèt and me on the couch for a snack. He'd just finished playing soccer with the neighborhood kids, who had been waiting for him in the yard when we arrived. Magga handed him a big piece of watermelon, which he devoured enthusiastically, placing his rind in the pile with the other discarded rinds, peels, and pits. Magga reached down and handed it back to him. She pointed to several pink patches still left on the rind. In broken English, she said with a smile, "Luke, you waste."

Luke nodded. He scraped off the remaining melon with his spoon. As I sat there watching this interaction, I thought of all the times I've made fruit salad, throwing out half the fruit with the rinds and peels because it was easier than taking the time to really scrape it off or cut carefully around a pit. I thought about our abundant life and how we took food for granted. We had no real concept of waste or hunger.

Our fruit salad production went on for hours. I sat in awe, watching the Dépestre women work their magic without food processors or cutting boards, hoping my visit would help me become more like them. Finally, Manmi Dèt gave the final stir, mixing together the thousands of orange, yellow, and red pieces of Haitian fruit we'd sliced and diced into a rainbow of color and texture. Magga's pineapple juice coated it all and glistened in the sun. We all stepped back to admire our work. This was the most magnificent fruit salad I'd ever seen—all the more so because of the loving way in which it was prepared.

Daily Mass with Manmi Dèt

Manmi Dèt and I left her house at four in the afternoon every weekday and walked through the neighborhood and up the steep hill to St. Clare's Church for Mass. Luke preferred to stay at home with Nennenn. There weren't any sidewalks, so we made our way in a zigzag pattern around dozens of one-room, concrete-block houses. This was our special time. Just the two of us. I looked forward to it each day.

Wearing colorful dresses she'd made herself, a matching hat, and low church heels, Manmi Dèt always dressed up for Mass. She held my hand the whole way and helped me navigate around broken glass, rusted cans, mud, discarded tires, and jagged pieces of concrete. As we passed her neighbors, she greeted everyone with an enthusiastic *"Bonjou!"* and a smile. *"Bonjou,* Manmi Dèt," they'd call back, waving. When she introduced me, I felt warmly received. If I was a friend of Manmi Dèt's, I was their friend.

The neighborhood felt calm and peaceful despite the rugged circumstances. There was a strong sense of community. Most everyone stood or sat outside their homes—all ages—chatting and watching the children. They all knew each other. The homes were so close together it wasn't clear whose property we were on as we passed through. I tried to peek inside the houses, but they were dark. Sometimes I made out a small wooden table and chair. I rarely saw anyone cooking or eating.

We often passed kids Luke's age kicking a deflated soccer ball around. I didn't see many toys or bikes, and never a stroller, a swing, or anything electronic like a Game Boy. We passed women squatting outside their homes, scrubbing clothes with a bar of soap and pail of water. How they got their clothes so clean was a mystery to me. On Sundays, when the church was packed, everyone's dresses, shirts, and pants showed no signs of the dust that seemed to fly everywhere and coat everything.

"Attention," Manmi Dèt would say in French, pointing out loose, slippery rocks. She'd tighten her grip and help me steady myself when I jumped over big pools of mud. When we got to one of Tiplas Kazo's main streets, Manmi Dèt would hold up her purse to shield us from the clouds of dust created by passing tap-taps and cars.

On the same corner every day, next to a family who sold grilled corn, waited Manmi Dèt's good friend, Irène. Irène had a radiant smile and a beautiful face that didn't show the stress of life in this city. She accompanied us up the final road to St. Clare's. It was steep, but Manmi Dèt and Irène were in amazing shape for women in their 70s. They didn't even break a sweat. When we finally arrived at the top of the hill and walked through the brown wooden doors of St. Clare's, it was close to 4:30.

We always sat in a pew in the front left section of the sanctuary, the exact spot I chose each Sunday growing up in my dad's church. There, waiting for us, were the same fifteen to twenty women, as though they'd never left. Faithful, committed, and holding their rosaries, they sat together and prayed every afternoon—some aloud, others silently. When Manmi Dèt arrived, the singing began.

Manmi Dèt had a great voice—not perfect in pitch, but strong and joyful. She loved singing and her enthusiasm encouraged everyone else to join in. There was no organ or piano, just these women singing *a cappella*. Manmi Dèt kept beat with her hand on the top of the pew in front of her. Sometimes they sang for fifteen minutes, sometimes an hour or more—it depended on when Fr. Gerry arrived. They just kept singing and praying until he walked out in his robe from behind the pulpit.

Not being Catholic or speaking Creole, I didn't understand most of the service, but the energy of the women around me was always uplifting. Just hearing Fr. Gerry's hopeful tone inspired me. Daily Mass became an important touchstone for me, a time to sit and feel.

The sanctuary was stiflingly hot. With no air-conditioning or even a fan, sweat poured down my face, neck, and back, mosquitoes always circling my ankles. After an hour or two, I'd get restless and thirsty, but I couldn't jump up to get a drink of water—there were no water fountains. So I just sat there in the heat, my mouth dry and my stomach grumbling, and tried to quiet my mind so I could be fully present.

This is one of the reasons I visit Haiti—to make it personal. To feel uncomfortable—physically and emotionally, so that I remember. In Berkeley when I get hot, I turn on a fan. If I feel cold, I turn on the heat or grab a sweater. Thirsty?

I turn on the faucet. Hungry? I open the refrigerator or go to the store. I never feel uncomfortable for more than a moment and can forget that these are real problems for others. Is being too comfortable one of the reasons the shade can be pulled down over an issue like world hunger, or hunger right in our own country? How can we get to a place where we care deeply about hunger or clean water—enough to act and make meaningful changes—when it's not personal? When we ourselves are never hungry or thirsty and don't actually see the suffering?

Mass always ended with the passionate prayer to St. Jude. I opened my palms and lifted my arms high above my head along with the other women. It didn't take me long to learn the words. As the prayer closed, the intensity built as the women cried out for help. They prayed fiercely day after day for Haiti, even though it didn't seem like the rest of the world ever heard them.

"Osekoooooooooouuuuuuuuuu." S.O.S.

Nighttime

M anmi Dèt's neighborhood didn't have streetlights, so at night the only light came from the moon. Bedtime was early for Luke and me, because the electricity was usually not working. We tried to use the dim lightbulb on the side of the wall that hooked up somehow to Nennenn's generator, to play cards or read, but it usually wasn't bright enough.

Our room was hot, making it difficult for me to fall asleep. Luke had no trouble. He was exhausted from playing soccer with the neighborhood kids and fell asleep as quickly as he did at home. I was relieved that he transitioned so smoothly into life at the Dépestres. He seemed comfortable with the heat, loved the food, enjoyed the new friends he was

making and the slow rhythm of his days. He didn't even com-
plain about the growing number of mosquito bites all over
his body. He was quiet when it came to talking about the living conditions of people in the neighborhood. I knew he was
taking it all in, and assumed he just hadn't found the words
to describe what he felt.

I often lay awake for hours listening to the sounds of the
neighborhood—dogs fighting, roosters crowing, people
singing at late-night church services, babies crying. Sometimes Manmi Dèt's daughter Nérie would come over to say
prayers with Manmi Dèt and Magga. I never actually saw
them, but I guessed they were sitting around a table in the
room just below me, perhaps with a candle between them.
Sometimes they'd pray for an hour, sometimes longer. They'd
start out quietly, whispering the rosary together, but then
Nérie's voice would rise as she shifted into other prayers. I
got chills as I listened. I couldn't understand a word, but the
passion and faith in her voice as she called out to the heav-
ens felt as though she was giving voice to the prayers of every
· hungry child and adult in Haiti.

Nighttime was a time for me to pray, too, and reflect on
what I was experiencing. My mind replayed the places and
people I'd seen. Each time I heard a child cry, I'd remember
the 18-month-old at the orphanage and all the children asleep
on dirt floors in Cité Soleil. A distant crack of thunder would
bring back the awful image of shacks in Cité Soleil flooding
with raw sewage after a heavy rain, and families having
nowhere to go.

Sweaty and restless, I'd think about what it must be like
for these children and their parents, but I could only let my
mind go so far. I couldn't imagine the heartache the mothers felt as they struggled to find food daily. To listen to their
children cry from hunger, to watch them die from starvation
or diarrhea. It was inconceivable to me. I listened to Luke's

breathing in the bed next to me and thought of our lives and how I'd never had to worry about these things, not even once. Someone told me that some of the mothers in Cité Soleil made clay biscuits for their children. It was all they had to feed them—dirt mixed with salt and vegetable shortening and baked in the sun.

When I couldn't sleep, I'd get up and lean on the window-sill and look out into the blackness. Sometimes a tropical breeze touched my face, reminding me of the nights I loved as a child when I visited my grandparents in the Cayman Islands, listening to the sound of waves and feeling the Caribbean breeze through my bedroom's screened window. I would spend my languid days playing in the sand, wading in the water, hunting for seashells, coconuts, and crabs. We went on picnics and I learned to snorkel. Every afternoon at 4:30, Grandma would serve fresh limeade from her tree and home-made chocolate chip cookies. My life had been idyllic and privileged.

Here in Port-au-Prince, even in the heat of a sleepless night, I lived in luxury compared to most Haitians. My toilet was hard to flush, but I had one. More than half of urban Haitians did not, and the percentage was much higher in the countryside. My lightbulb hardly lit the room, but I had electricity and a backup generator. Only a third of urban Haitians had electricity in their homes, and a fraction had generators. Again, the statistics were much worse in the countryside. I had my own room with a bed, sheet, and pillow. I ate two or three meals every day. I had plenty of bottled water and access to Nennenn's cold-water shower. I had toilet paper and tampons.

Plus, I would be getting on a plane in a few weeks to fly back to the Bay Area, to my house with wood floors, painted walls, and furniture in every room. I had lamps and a computer, a full refrigerator and hot showers, a closet full of clothes and a car in my driveway. I had an education, a job, a doctor, and a dentist. I had everything I needed to live in comfort. The contrast was overwhelming. How could I reconcile the imbalance? I couldn't. And what could be done to balance the vast inequalities in the world? In Haiti, I'd come face-to-face with the world's poorest citizens—and knew they were part of the one billion people on our planet who live in extreme poverty, those who don't have access to the basic needs for survival. I struggled with this reality and didn't know what to do about it. These thoughts kept me awake at night.

Bòn Fèt

Luke turned 9 on a Thursday. A surprise care package from a friend in Chicago arrived earlier in the week with party supplies—cake mix, frosting, candles, hats, and balloons. Early in the morning, Luke woke up, excited about the celebration we'd planned for the afternoon. Berry Philippe, Daphné, and a few other kids from St. Clare's met us on Manmi Dèt's porch at two o'clock. *"Bòn fèt, Luke!"* they shouted in unison.

A game of catch started out the party. The kids eagerly carried the bags of donated baseball gear into the yard. They each put on a jersey and cap and cracked up laughing as they practiced catching the ball in the glove. Baseball was big in the Dominican Republic, but it wasn't played in Haiti. Soccer was the main sport.

Next was batting practice. Luke positioned a tee in the driveway, put a tennis ball on it, and took a big demonstration swing. I was afraid someone might get hurt with the bat, but I stayed in the background and let them play. Luke knew only a handful of Creole words. The Haitian kids knew about the same amount of English. But it seemed effortless for them to come together, share, cooperate, and have fun.

After an hour, Luke ran upstairs to get the soccer ball we'd brought.

"G - Ò - Ò - Ò - Ò - Ò - Ò - Ò - Ò - Ò - Ò - L!"

"Goal" must be a universal word because they all screamed it at the same time when the ball made its way through the two chairs positioned as goal markers in Manmi Dèt's yard.

Finally, sweaty and tired, the kids collapsed on the porch. Luke brought out a box of Knex, a Lego-like toy, which they eagerly examined. There were at least 100 small pieces, which, once assembled, would become a helicopter. Luke and I had tried several times to put it together, but it was too complicated. We'd followed the directions page by page, but still couldn't get everything to fit together properly. The kids poured all the pieces in a pile on the porch. I watched them stare at the box and then at the pieces. Once in a while they consulted the diagrams in the directions. Within fifteen minutes, they had assembled the helicopter, perfectly.

The water balloon toss was the highlight of the party. Balloons flew around the yard. Screams. Laughter. Loud pops. Then chocolate cake. Nennenn baked it in her oven, the first time I ever saw her use it. Manmi Dèt and Magga joined as we gathered around the table to sing "Happy Birthday"—first in English, then in Creole, then in French. The cake was cut and put into the palms of our hands. I watched the kids savor every bite. Berry Philippe licked the frosting off his fingers and smiled. I imagined it had been a long time since he'd had chocolate.

As the day ended, Luke beamed as he waved good-bye to his friends. He looked older to me. Maybe it was the way he carried himself. Maybe it was a depth I saw in his eyes. He'd been exposed to poverty and hunger, and the privilege of experiencing another family in an intimate way. He loved Nennenn's rice and beans, playing Go Fish with Daphné, and soccer with Berry Philippe and his friends. He had watched Manmi Dèt teach the neighborhood kids math on the green chalkboard tied to her porch railing, and sewing, with her foot-pedal machine. He felt confident walking to the corner store to buy his favorite Haitian cola—asking for it in Creole and paying for it with Haitian coins. Although he found church a little boring, he sat through many St. Clare Masses, observing the congregation's faith, taking in their music and Fr. Gerry's passionate sermons. He was welcomed by the parishioners with kisses and hugs. This is why I brought him to Haiti, to experience another culture and put his own life in perspective.

Muumuu

When I packed for this trip, I put two pairs of sandals, five sundresses, and one skirt and blouse for Mass in my suitcase. I had learned on my previous visits to Port-au-Prince that Haitian women usually don't wear pants or shorts. I didn't bring any makeup or a hairdryer. Only one pair of earrings. My theme was simplicity.

What became my favorite dress was a light-blue-and-white faded muumuu with pink lace trim that Manmi Dèt made for me. Not my usual style, but I loved it, even though it made me look pregnant. With daily temperatures in the upper 90s, the muumuu was perfect. Oversized, lightweight, sleeveless, hemmed just below the knee. My unshaven shins and armpits were exposed, but after a few days I didn't care. I felt raw and liberated.

I always wore my muumuu on Sundays after the food program. After a long day of preparing and serving the meal, slipping into it felt cool and comforting. The fabric was worn and soft and seemed to hold the love Manmi Dèt had sewn into it when she made it for me.

I liked to spend Sunday evenings relaxing at Nennenn's house. We'd pull a couple of straw chairs out to her porch and settle back to enjoy the stars and catch a breeze. Leaning back in our muumuus, we'd have a glass of cold water and chat about the day. Sundays were bittersweet—the satisfaction of seeing hundreds of children fed, combined with the sadness of the reality of their daily hunger.

One particularly hot and humid Sunday in late July, even in my muumuu, I was dripping with sweat.

"Let's go for a swim," Nennenn suggested, pointing to her new pool. It was tiny—about 12 feet by 8 feet—but full of refreshing water.

"I'll get my suit," I said.

"No, Margo. Just go in your dress."

Swim in my muumuu? Nennenn took my hand and pulled me out of my chair, laughing as she ran to the pool. "Come on. Jump in."

She was in the water in a flash, her purple muumuu floating around her. I hesitated, remembering all the insects and algae that lived in the pool. It didn't have a filtering system and the water wasn't changed very often. Oh, why not? What's a little fungus? I thought. Plunging in—underwear, muumuu, and all—I felt about 8 years old. I don't remember ever going swimming with my clothes on intentionally, even as a kid.

Nennenn and I laughed hysterically, not able to stop for the longest time. Suddenly, my eyes overflowed with tears, my mouth quivered, and my chest heaved as I laughed and cried at the same time. It surprised me. I wasn't sure where the tears came from. It had been ages since I'd had so much fun. I couldn't remember the last time. Somehow life had gotten so serious. And it was serious, especially in Haiti. The food program earlier that day had shown me that again. But it was more than that.

Maybe I was crying because I was overwhelmed by the love of the Dépestre family and the beauty of simple things like a soft faded muumuu and a plunge in the water with a dear friend. Or maybe because I was discovering more and more how unfair the world is, how cruel it can be. The disparity between my life and the lives of everybody I met in Tiplas Kazo weighed on me all the time. Feelings of joy and grief wove themselves throughout my days in Haiti. Little by little they seeped out, growing in intensity as the days passed. But in the pool they spilled over, soaking my already wet face with tears.

Nennenn and I settled side by side on the pool step with water up to our necks and our muumuus ballooning around us. We leaned our heads back and looked up at the stars. It had been quite a day.

As I stared at the night sky, a dream I'd had after Rich died came to mind. It was more like a visitation than a dream. It felt as real and clear as my time with Nennenn in the pool. In it, Rich handed me a letter about my past, present, and future. I knew it answered all my questions about his death and "why," but I couldn't decipher his handwriting, except for two words, written boldly and clearly at the bottom of the page: "Live life."

Swimming in my muumuu under the stars after a full day in Tiplas Kazo, experiencing a full range of emotions, I felt as if I was moving on and growing strong in my own life, separate from him. My heart was healing and felt full and alive with the food program, the Dépestres, Fr. Gerry, and every-one at St. Clare's. I felt I was finally starting to do what he'd asked of me: Live life.

St. Jude's Chapel

*A*llo, allo, hello," Fr. Gerry said as he enthusiastically an-swered his cell phone. It rang often. I spent many days driving with him in his jeep from place to place and was amazed by his energy and ability to coordinate dozens of projects. His parish stretched for miles, and he felt a re-sponsibility to all the people in it. I wondered if he ever slept.

In addition to the daily Mass at St. Clare's, he hosted a weekly national call-in radio program. It was lively and pop-ular and covered social and political issues. Nennenn and Toto listened to it every Saturday on Radio Ginen during the long drive to market. He'd also been busy that summer plan-ning a neighborhood party on the rectory grounds. There would be a band and dancing and hundreds of people. He told me Tiplas Kazo needed things to look forward to that would bring a sense of community, joy, and fun. A group of St. Clare's teenagers he'd been encouraging, called the "young entrepreneurs," would kick off a new soda-selling business at the event. In the midst of all of this, he was training a new group of altar girls and a dozen confirmands. He visited the sick and elderly, and said Mass for the Missionaries of Char-ity nuns at the orphanage. He always found time to greet the neighborhood children and pass out jellybeans.

"See what it takes to make a Haitian child happy, Mar-garet?" he'd say every time.

On one afternoon, he invited me to go with him to cele-brate the first Mass at a new chapel a few miles from St. Clare's. Overseeing construction projects was another part of his day. I imagined his degree in engineering really came in handy. He'd named the chapel St. Jude. The people it was going to serve lived too far from St. Clare's to walk to Mass, so building a place for them to worship had been a dream of his for years. Now it was a reality. The first Mass would start in an hour.

When we got to the site of the new chapel, Fr. Gerry jumped out of the jeep, walked down a steep path of rocks, and exclaimed, "Here it is!"

I looked where he pointed, but didn't see anything but a concrete shell—a floor, one wall, and a ceiling held up by exposed metal poles. The construction site was surrounded by small concrete-block homes. An old faded skirt and blouse were drying on a wood railing just a few feet away.

"Where is it?" I whispered, embarrassed to ask.

"Right here," he said matter-of-factly as he stepped onto a smooth surface in the midst of piles of concrete blocks and rubble. Stretching his arms over his head, he let out one of his belly laughs and announced, "The St. Jude Chapel is finally here!" Then he spun around in a circle, beaming, and said, "We poured the floor yesterday. It's dry now."

As I stood in the middle of the small floor and looked around at the empty space, women in Sunday dresses, hats, and shoes started to arrive, bringing rickety chairs from their homes a few yards away. They lined them up carefully to form pews. A young man set up a card table on the edge of the floor. Then an elderly woman carefully smoothed a pretty white tablecloth over it. Fr. Gerry put on his robe and then reverently placed his Bible and communion cup on the table. A teenager sitting on a cinder block started beating a drum between his legs, signaling the start of the opening hymn.

Fr. Gerry led the Mass with the same love and intensity he always did at St. Clare's. Whether there were 700 people or a handful, I didn't see any difference in the way he prayed, preached, or reverently lifted the communion cup. Here we were in his new open-air chapel with no pews, no windows, no doors, only a wooden cross leaning on a pile of rocks.

The Man in the Street

Nennenn wanted to buy sewing supplies for Manmi Dèt after our weekly stop at the farmers' market, so we went deeper into the city than usual. I'd been to this part of town once before, when Fr. Gerry and I drove to get paint for Paul.

When we got to the fabric store, I decided to stay in the car and wait while Nennenn and Toto ran in. Just a few seconds passed before a little girl walked up to my window. She held out her hand and touched her belly. Her eyes pleaded with me. I didn't have any money with me, so I apologized in French, *"Je regrette de ne pouvoir vous aider."* She walked away, disappointed. A minute later, another child walked up. This time it was a boy, no more than 6 or 7 years old, with a frayed Chuck E. Cheese T-shirt. As our eyes met and I tried to tell him I didn't have any money with me, I thought about Bryan's song, the one I'd heard years ago about the restaurant and the meal and the waiter pulling the shade down. Here was that hungry boy on the other side of my car window. We were only inches from each other and I couldn't pull the shade down. But I couldn't help him either. He stuffed his hands in his empty pockets and walked away.

My head pounded, and I started to feel depressed. I'd been protected staying in Manmi Dèt's neighborhood. Life for the children in Tiplas Kazo was difficult, but they had a strong community, and there was Fr. Gerry, St. Clare's, and the meals on Sundays. Here, in the heart of the city, it felt raw and overwhelming. So many people struggling to make a living. So many children begging for help.

Nennenn came back with a small bag of supplies, and we continued on our way. I was relieved to be moving again. But just a block or two later, the car stopped. We sat for several minutes and then finally inched forward. As we approached the intersection, I could tell that cars were driving around something. I leaned forward to see what was happening and fell back wishing I'd never looked. A middle-aged man was lying facedown in the middle of the street. Clearly, he was dead.

Maybe he'd collapsed from starvation. Maybe a car had hit him. Maybe he'd been shot. He looked like he had just been walking across the street. Why wasn't anyone doing anything? No ambulance. No police. Part of me wanted to jump out and run to him, move him to the curb and place a blanket or jacket or something over him. Another part was too scared to do anything. I had been sheltered my whole life. I'd never seen a dead person in the street before. Nennenn placed her hand over mine as we took a left and drove down a side street away from the congestion. I could tell from her reaction that things like this happened every day.

I closed my eyes and slumped down, leaning my head against the backseat.

"Margo, are you okay?" Nennenn asked, smoothing the bangs off my forehead.

"I'm just tired," I lied. I felt increasingly weak and sick, with the urge to run. A dead man. Dozens of begging children. Thoughts swirled, giving me a pounding headache.

I was a 39-year-old white, middle-class woman who didn't speak Creole, had never studied Haitian history or politics or global economics or grassroots organizing or fund-raising or anything like that. I didn't know what I was doing. The problems were too huge. The number of people in need was too large.

My worries spun out of control.

The food program fed a handful of children one meal a week. It was just a drop. A Band-Aid. Plus, there was no guarantee the money was going to keep coming in. Telling a few family members and friends was not enough. What would happen if the money ran out and the food program had to end? I'd be seen as another naïve *blan* do-gooder who created expectations she couldn't meet. Who didn't know what she was doing. A failure. Besides, I wasn't doing anything to address the reasons they were hungry in the first place, which I knew was the key to change.

My throat was tight. I struggled to hold back tears so Nennenn wouldn't notice. I hated what I was thinking, but couldn't stop myself. I didn't belong here. I should get Luke and leave right now, this afternoon. There'd been a dead man in the street, for God's sake. And there were probably hundreds of others. It wasn't safe! There had to be resentment under the surface toward a visiting American. The U.S. government had played a big role throughout history in why the poor are so poor in Haiti. Cité Soleil was packed with misery. It could explode any minute. Another violent coup was always a possibility. My family and friends were right. Luke should be in Little League, not under mosquito netting. He was only 9. I was in way over my head. Fr. Gerry would understand. Manmi Dèt and Nennenn would understand. There was probably a flight to Miami in a few hours. Luke and I could be on it.

Empty Pots

When I returned to Manmi Dèt's house and saw her reassuring smile as she carefully chopped cabbage for the Sunday meal, my fears slowly dissolved. So instead of packing my bags, I picked up a peeler and joined her.

At noon the next day, hundreds of boys and girls gathered at the rectory, waiting patiently in the burning sun for their turn to sit at the table. Nennenn's creation smelled particularly delicious. The children fidgeted, squealed, and hopped up and down with anticipation of the feast that was coming their way. I leaned against the cement wall in the kitchen and watched Nennenn and her faithful crew of women scoop out generous portions from their huge pots. Gravy overflowed the sides of the plates. Most well-fed Americans wouldn't be able to finish one of these servings. But I knew that here, even the tiniest child would eat every last drop, like a camel storing away water.

As I looked at all the food and the steady stream of plates being passed down the volunteer line, I remembered a conversation I'd had with Nennenn when I'd visited with Paul.

"Do you ever worry on Sundays that you won't have enough?" I had asked.

She smiled. "Many times, it's like Jesus and the bread and the fish. Sometimes when I put the food on the plate, I see the pot never empties. The food ... expands."

"Until the last child is fed?" I'd asked, amazed.

"Yes."

"Like the loaves and fishes miracle," I whispered.

She nodded. "Yes, Margo. Giving food is miracle."

The serving went on until 2:30. Finally, the crowd of children cleared and it appeared that everyone had been fed. The volunteers settled into their meals. Berry Philippe squatted next to me and dived into his stew with a big spoon. He ate quickly at first, but then slowed down, savoring every bite. When he finished, he leaned back against the wall, patted his belly, and smiled.

Suddenly, I heard loud voices outside the kitchen yelling something to the cooks. Nennenn shouted back a response in Creole I didn't understand. It didn't sound like an argument, but I knew it was serious.

In a flash, the kitchen was full of people—mostly adults in their 20s and 30s, but there were a few children too. With hands outstretched, they pushed toward the empty pots. Their voices begged for a meal. Nennenn motioned for them to leave. She said there wasn't any more food. They pressed forward.

My heart beat wildly with panic. I was afraid a fight might break out. *Where are you, God?* I cried out in my mind. How could we run out of food at this crucial moment? What about the loaves and fishes miracle? It's happened other Sundays. Why not today? Nennenn and the other servers dug into the bottom of the pots and pans, scraping hard to find something to give the crowd. I watched a woman with sunken cheeks reach out her hand in desperation. Thankfully, Nennenn found a small bit of burned rice and dropped it into her palm. The woman instantly gobbled it up.

A tiny girl in a yellow dress gripped her mother's hand tightly as she was pulled into the kitchen. Pressed against all the other bodies, she looked at me and smiled. Her eyes were playful. Then she hid her head behind her mother's leg and popped out the other side. Peekaboo! Peekaboo in the middle of all this chaos? I tried to smile back, but I was too scared to play with her. I stood on tiptoe to see if Nennenn could find anything to give her mother, but every last bit of rice was gone. The little girl's bright eyes never left mine until she crossed the threshold and disappeared into the dusty street with all the others, empty-handed.

Here to Love

I climbed up the stairs exhausted, crawled under my mosquito netting, and tried to sleep. First the orphans, then the dead man, then we ran out of food. My fears returned, this time with more strength. We couldn't feed all the children who found their way to the rectory. We'd never be able to feed them all. And with the world the way it is, they will always be hungry. When Luke came to bed, I was glad the electricity was off again so he couldn't see me crying into my pillow. The distant cries of babies reminded me of the many others who couldn't sleep either.

In the next few days, I had no energy to practice my Creole, no desire to play with Luke or the neighborhood children, no interest in hanging out with Nennenn or riding around with Fr. Gerry. I pretended to be reading, but my eyes couldn't focus on the page. Images played over and over in my mind—the dead man, the little girl in the yellow dress, the woman with sunken cheeks eating rice out of her hand. The only thing I felt like doing was walking to Mass with Manmi Dèt. Since we spoke so little of each other's language, it was easy to be with her. Most of the time, we shared a comfortable silence.

That Wednesday, Mass didn't start at 4:30. Fr. Gerry was delayed, so Manmi Dèt led the singing while we waited. Instead of following along in the songbook as I usually did, I glanced over my shoulder at Paul's painting of Jesus, hoping that his image would inspire me. Where was the hope, I wondered. Where was the help? It didn't seem that anyone heard the Haitian cry of *"Osekooooooooooouuuuuuu."* Our little food program had been swallowed up by the need. It was just too small and the problem was too big. The situation was desperate, and, it seemed, getting worse by the day. Staring at the Jesus painting, I asked, *Why am I here?* and waited for an answer.

I didn't hear anything except Manmi Dèt's voice and the pounding of her hand on the top of the pew. I fidgeted in my seat. I felt hot, depressed, and mad at myself for crumpling under pressure. I couldn't seem to access anything I'd learned from Fr. Gerry's *piti piti* wisdom.

The memory of the little girl playing peekaboo and then disappearing out the kitchen door empty-handed wouldn't leave me. *See!* I cried out in my mind. *I couldn't feed her. I can't do it.*

You're here to love.

The thought was just a whisper, but I heard it clearly. I turned around and looked at the painting again.

Fr. Gerry unexpectedly spoke in English. My mind snapped to attention. I hadn't realized he'd arrived. He was in the middle of his welcome but it wasn't in Creole. He was talking to me, which he had done in a service on only one other occasion. "...and we thank you, Margaret, for coming to Haiti to be with us. We thank you and all the benefactors in the U.S. who are helping us feed some of Haiti's hungry children. We are glad you are here with us, in solidarity, Margaret."

Fr. Gerry was welcoming me so warmly. The women in the pews were smiling and nodding and patting my arm and shoulder. Yes, they were glad I was there—even though I could help with just one meal a week for only a few hundred children, even though there was no guarantee of whether we'd have enough food to feed them all, even though I didn't know how to address the underlying reasons they were hungry in the first place, even though I was going to leave them in a few weeks and go back to my house and car and full refrigerator and my life that was so packed with comforts and conveniences.

As I sat with Manmi Dèt, listening to her pray and sing, I started to think that maybe I wasn't an impostor. It wasn't about quantity or effectiveness or our different lives. It was simpler than that. It was about solidarity. It was about love. On that afternoon, in the front left pew, the words "You're here to love" became my guide. I promised to myself to remember those words whenever I got swept up in the complexity of numbers and money and expectations and worry. I'd remember Berry Philippe and his smile as he dipped his spoon in his bowl. I knew the value of even one meal.

Pase Yon Bon Moman

Manmi Dèt said she wanted me to go to the beach. I love sand and surf—something about large bodies of water makes me feel calm and at peace—but the beach was never a place I expected to visit in Haiti. On a Saturday morning, Magga and Daphné packed a bag lunch and some towels, and we piled into the brown jeep—Dede, Magga, Nancy, Luke, Daphné, and Carla, Manmi Dèt's niece, who had just arrived from Cleveland for a visit, and me. The beach we were going to was a two-hour drive away.

After four tries, the jeep's engine turned over and started to chug. I rolled down my window and waved to Manmi Dèt, Nennenn, and Fayla, Manmi Dèt's sister, who had come with Carla from Ohio. They stayed behind to work on the Sunday meal. Just as we rounded the corner, Fayla waved and called out in English, "Margo, have a good moment."

"*Mèsi*, Fayla," I called back, soaking in her good-bye. I'd never heard that expression before.

Just outside the city, as the sky seemed to expand and the barren mountain range came into full view, we pulled over to buy two stalks of sugarcane from a street merchant. We each broke off a piece and sucked on the sweet cane juice as we bounced down the narrow road. Dede's speedometer was broken, so I don't know how fast we were going—probably not more than 15 miles an hour because of all the potholes and rocks. But I didn't mind the slow drive. It gave me time to take in the countryside.

A toothless man carrying a machete nodded in acknowledgment as we drove by his wooden house. Young girls carrying plastic jugs chatted as they walked alongside the road to gather precious water. Boys played marbles in dusty yards. Occasionally we'd pass a family selling cassavas or mangoes.

The villages we drove through were tiny, only a handful of houses in each, and I wondered where the children went to school and how the families got their cooking oil, rice, beans, clothes, or tools. I imagined they had to go to Port-au-Prince or walk for miles to a larger town. I didn't see any electrical lines or telephone wires. The level of poverty looked the same as in Port-au-Prince, but there was a wonderful feeling of spaciousness and clean air. Despite the vast deforestation, there were banana and plantain groves, a hint of the tropical paradise Haiti once was. The villages seemed peaceful and I imagined if given the choice, many Port-au-Prince residents would prefer to live in the countryside if they could feed their families and send their children to school.

Every once in a while, we stopped to allow a family of roosters and hens to pass. I saw a few farmers trying to break the hard ground with a spade. I don't know how they watered their plots of land, but in some places, I saw seedlings breaking through the harsh earth.

After two hours, we arrived at the white sandy beach, and we were the only ones there. It was state-owned and required a small fee, prohibitive to most Haitians. The water was a smattering of turquoise blue and emerald green, clear and warm. Mountains with jagged cliffs surrounded us. The beach reminded me of the Cayman Islands or Mexico—breathtakingly beautiful—except that it was empty.

We swam and splashed and ate watermelon and bread with jam. As I sat on my wooden beach chair and watched Luke and Daphné play in the waves, Fayla's words, "Have a good moment," sung in my ears. I asked Carla about the translation, and she said that her mother had translated word for word the Creole expression *"Pase yon bon moman,"* which was used like our "Have a good day."

That night the whole family gathered at the house of Manmi Dèt's daughter Marjorie to talk about the beach. Marjorie lived with her husband and 5-year-old daughter just a few feet through the trees. Without TV, computers, or phones, there always was time to gather and talk. This was a big part of Haitian life and it was precious.

If there are such things as past lives, I must have been a member of the Dépestre family. Being with them was so natural and easy for me. Our trip to the beach in the jeep reminded me of trips my family took in our station wagon, all seven of us piling in, to spend a day out of Chicago.

Feeling tired after all the sun, I was ready to turn in for the night when Marjorie pulled out a boom box, turned on some Haitian music, and started dancing. The music had an infectious Caribbean beat. Nennenn joined in. Then Nérie. Their hips moved in sync with the drums, their movements fluid and graceful, beautiful to watch. They looked so comfortable in their bodies. I sat in awe as they twirled and laughed, their skirts swinging.

"Come on, Margo. You too." I tried to resist, telling them I didn't really know how to dance, but they pulled me out of my chair. "It's easy. Just feel the music and move your hips."

Easy for them to say. My hips didn't shake like theirs. They were stiff, almost stuck. The sisters laughed playfully as they watched me try to copy them. "Don't think, Margo. Just move to the rhythm. Relax. Have fun."

Don't think. Have fun. Those are two of the hardest things for me to do. *Pase yon bon moman,* I reminded myself. Nennenn took my hands and guided my steps. Slowly I started to relax. I closed my eyes and tried to feel the music. Within a few minutes, it was working its magic, as my muscles loosened and thoughts of how silly I looked evaporated. My hips began to sway and my arms flung from side to side. It was great fun. Nennenn clapped with excitement. "You're getting it, Margo. Good. Good. Just like a Haitian sister."

We danced in a circle under the stars, sweat dripping down our faces and backs. As we twirled and laughed, my throat started to tighten and my eyes welled up with tears. It was as though emotions trapped in my body were being released. Like the night in Nennenn's pool, feelings of both joy and grief overwhelmed me. I fought to hold them back, afraid that once they started, they wouldn't stop. I was so happy, and so sad. Allowing myself to laugh and dance seemed to unlock the full range of feelings that had accumulated since my first trip to Haiti—the tears I couldn't cry when I first arrived, tears for the butterfly lady and the other women at Son Fils, tears for the babies at the orphanage and Cité Soleil, tears for all the children who are hungry, and the incredible joy of feeling the love from the St. Clare's community. Emotions of each extreme lived within me and it seemed the more I let go, the more I felt them.

The music ended and we kissed each other good night. As Nennenn kissed my cheek, she whispered in my ear, "Dancing is good for you, Margo."

Giving and Receiving

It was the last Sunday of my visit. Boys and girls dressed in their best clothes danced and clapped to the beat of an old trumpet as they waited patiently outside the rectory door. The St. Clare's neighborhood was abuzz with the anticipation of another meal.

I helped unload the jeep, carrying pots and plates into the kitchen. Manmi Dèt and Irène were already positioned, ready to dish up the hot rice and stew. When the door opened, the youngest children ran into the front rooms and slid into position on the benches. Fr. Gerry greeted them in his red-and-white-striped apron. He squeezed into the middle of a packed bench in the main room and began a chant.

"Jezi te di bay timoun yo manje."

Over and over the children repeated the sentence, playfully pounding their fists on the table. Fr. Gerry laughed and encouraged them to shout out the sentence even louder. Soon everyone in the rectory joined in.

"Jezi te di bay timoun yo manje."

After the children started eating and the room quieted, I asked Fr. Gerry what they were saying.

"Oh, they love this chant. They're crying out, 'Jesus said to feed the children. Jesus said to feed the children.'" He laughed and took a bite of rice and beans. "They deserve to eat, Margaret. Jesus said, 'I was hungry and you fed me.' That's what we're doing here. We're feeding the children and God is so happy and so are the children. Look at them!"

The room was packed with kids digging into their food. Hundreds more waited anxiously outside the front door. Overflowing plates streamed down the line of volunteers and up the stairs to the second floor. With the trumpet outside still belting out tunes, it felt like a celebration.

"It's greater giving than receiving, Margaret, don't you think?" Fr. Gerry said as he finished his plate. "A person would rather be the giver. But sometimes you're born in a country where you're put in a position to receive. Others are born in a country in a better position to give. Both the giver and receiver need each other. The giver can sleep at night because she has the satisfaction that comes with giving. The receiver can sleep at night, too, because his belly is full."

I thought about all the What If? Foundation donors and what their giving had resulted in. Hundreds of full bellies. But their giving had also created the opportunity for more giving. The faces of the people in the packed kitchen and in the shoulder-to-shoulder chain of plate-passers were lit up with the joy that comes from serving others. We needed each other to give. The donors' gifts wouldn't result in full bellies unless the St. Clare's members also gave their time and love.

Fr. Gerry pointed to the fifty adults waiting in the sun in hopes there would be food left over for them. Some were elderly and frail. Others were young adults. "This community would like to participate in the life of this country and the rest of the world. They want to give. They want to contribute. They would like to have their share in education, their share in infrastructure, their share of work, their share in health care. Many of them think they've been forgotten by everyone except by God, who's sent some messengers— some friends to help them meet their basic needs." He patted my shoulder and returned to St. Clare's for a meeting.

When all the children had finished eating, I felt tense, waiting to see if there would be enough food to feed the adults standing in the yard. I was more emotionally prepared for the possibility we'd run out again, reminding myself to focus on love and *piti piti*. But I didn't want to see them walk home disappointed. One old man looked as if he would pass out if he didn't eat soon. I looked at Nennenn sitting in front of a huge pot. She kept reaching in with her spoon and more rice kept coming out. The plates were flowing out of the kitchen. On that day, everybody ate.

As I watched the children and adults file out of the rectory grounds into the dusty street, I tried to capture every detail so I'd remember it when I returned to Berkeley. Gabriel Joseph, a student who lived on the second floor of the rectory, walked out of the kitchen and joined me. He looked up to the sky, put both hands on his belly, and sighed. Gabriel spoke English, so he had been an invaluable translator during the Sunday meals.

"We don't know how to thank you, Margo, for this food," he said, looking at me earnestly. "I don't have anything I can give you. We don't have anything to give you, we are so poor. But . . . " He smiled and his eyes sparkled. "We can pray. And we do, every day. We pray for you and for all the people who are giving us this food. Prayer is what we can give you, because we want to give you something back."

I thought about the gift of prayer flowing out of St. Clare's to all the donors. They didn't even know they were receiving it. And I thought about all the other intangible gifts I'd received from my Haitian friends. My heart ached with the thought of leaving them in a few days. The giving and receiving flowed between us continuously. To me, the two felt balanced, one part not more important than the other. We needed each other.

Map Tounen

The plane lifted off the runway and, within seconds, Port-au-Prince disappeared under the clouds. Luke's hand was in mine, as it always was during takeoffs and landings. In ninety minutes we'd be in Miami. Staring out my window, I didn't see the dark blue sea below, but instead saw the faces of Fr. Gerry, Manmi Dèt, and Nennenn. I didn't want to say good-bye when I left—it felt so final—so instead I used one of the Creole phrases I'd learned, *"Map tounen"*— I'll be back.

I loved the Dépestre family and all the people at St. Clare's. Spending nearly eight weeks in their community had cemented my connection to them. Knowing I'd be back many more times made my departure easier. I was already thinking about when I might return.

The flight attendant brought us a turkey sandwich, juice, and a cookie, and Luke dived in. He was ready to go home. He missed his friends and was excited about starting third grade. But he loved the Dépestres, too, and said he was happy we spent the summer in Haiti. I knew our time in Port-au-Prince had been one of the most important things I'd done for him.

I didn't feel like eating. The food placed in front of me only reminded me of the children in Tiplas Kazo who could never fly out of Haiti on a plane. I stared at the clouds and prayed I would never forget their hunger, that their daily prayer to St. Jude would always sing in my ears—*"Ose-koooooooooouuuuuu"*—and that, one day, their cry of S.O.S. wouldn't be needed.

As I looked at the sweets on my tray, I remembered the "powder of love" coconut treat and smiled, picturing Nennenn mixing the ingredients, Nancy patiently spooning the mixture into 500 tiny bags, and Manmi Dèt tying each bag carefully at the top. I thought about the importance of *Pase yon bon moman*. I'd never felt more grounded or present, thanks to their gentle guidance and example.

I leaned my head against the seat and closed my eyes, trying to remember more details. I could see Manmi Dèt peeling eggplants, protected from the scorching sun by the awning, and Nancy rubbing lime on each piece of chicken. I saw Nennenn and the careful way she watched over every pot, tasting with a wooden spoon and adding her delicious spices. Then the way Irène balanced overflowing plates of rice and stew and placed them on the kitchen ledge. I would never forget the look of satisfaction and relief on Berry Philippe's face as he dipped his spoon into his plate of food.

The meal at St. Clare's had become so much more than I could ever have imagined—from Fr. Gerry's original vision of feeding the children to a celebration feast every Sunday, fueled by love.

As the plane approached Miami, I braced myself for the shock of reentry into life in the U.S. What would the future hold for the What If? Foundation? I didn't have a detailed plan. I wasn't even sure what the next step would be. *"Piti piti."* I heard Fr. Gerry's words in my head. Little by little. One step at a time. Then I had an image of Fr. Gerry at the first Mass at St. Jude's, standing on the freshly poured cement floor, his white robe blowing in the breeze, his arms outstretched, and a smile on his face. He reminded me I don't have to have it all figured out. *Piti piti na rive.*

Epilogue

Nearly seven years have passed since the summer Luke and I spent in Port-au-Prince. I've been back to visit many times. The summer of 2001 remains fresh in my mind, fueling the lifelong commitment I have to the children in Tiplas Kazo.

The years since then have been extremely difficult for Fr. Gerry and the members of St. Clare's. Their prayer to St. Jude has grown stronger and stronger as families struggled to survive through an aid embargo, a coup d'état, and the current global food crisis that has sent rice prices soaring and created a near famine throughout Haiti.

In 2001, international loans to the Haitian government worth hundreds of millions of dollars were blocked, including $500 million in preapproved support for health care, education, potable water, and road improvement. The U.S. government led the loan freeze. A minor electoral dispute regarding eight parliamentary seats (out of 7,500 total offices) in the May 2000 elections was cited as the reason. But even though seven of the senators in question resigned in 2001, and the term of the eighth expired shortly thereafter, the blockade did not end until 2004.

The toll on the population was devastating. Inflation skyrocketed and the economy collapsed. Throughout the aid embargo, Haiti was required to pay millions of dollars in interest on some of the frozen loans—even though the country had not received them! This, combined with other debt payments, left the Aristide government with few resources to improve the lives of the poor majority.

Throughout this period, Nennenn, Manmi Dèt, and others from St. Clare's never missed a single Sunday afternoon serving meals at the rectory, and the number of children fed increased during this time from 500 to 750. The What If? Foundation also started a small education fund to pay for scholarships, beginning with ten students in September 2002. In 2003, a summer arts & crafts camp was organized, initiated by Manmi Dèt and Nennenn. Fr. Gerry's guidance, *"Piti piti,"* helped me stay focused and hopeful.

Then, in February 2004, there was a coup d'état and things got even worse. Former members of the Haitian military (which had been demobilized by Aristide in 1995) marched through the country. President Aristide received no help from the U.S. or other international powers to preserve his democratically elected government and was, instead, forced onto a plane and taken out of the country and into exile by U.S. military personnel.

Immediately following the coup, U.S. Marines entered and occupied Haiti. An interim government, backed by the U.S., was installed. Its police force targeted supporters of President Aristide and his Lavalas party. The jails, which had been emptied during the coup, freeing even convicted death-squad leaders, were quickly filled with political prisoners. Fr. Gerry e-mailed me reports on the crisis and its impact on the community:

> It is a tough place to live in these days. The new de facto government cannot satisfy the urgent basic needs of the population. It is becoming panicky. Armed criminals, [who] escaped from jails during the coup, are running the streets causing insecurity ... People are going hungry and are putting a lot of pressure on the new de facto government. The assistance promised has not been delivered. The

public workers cannot be paid. The trash remains uncollected. No water from the State company. No more electricity. Lack of money, claim the new officials . . . We have lost some of our basic rights, such as freedom of speech, freedom of assembly, particularly in the evening. People are scared. I also feel the pressure. If our food program was not taking place, Tiplas Kazo could become like downtown Port-au-Prince, where living is impossible for all. I have to preach louder and give more services. My heart is bleeding for the people . . . May more of us on the face of the earth hear the call of Jesus through Matthew 25 . . . God's blessing always!

Gerry

A few weeks after the coup, we took a leap of faith and started a meal on Wednesdays. We had collected enough donations to pay for stoves in the St. Clare's rectory, and tables, benches, and a roof for the "outdoor cafeteria" Fr. Gerry had envisioned years earlier, so a second cooking crew from St. Clare's was lined up. Although we were not sure if there would be enough money to keep the second meal going more than a few months, we started anyway.

In June 2004, U.S. troops began to withdraw and were replaced by multinational UN forces. Repression of Aristide supporters continued. More than a thousand opponents of the new regime were jailed. Fr. Gerry, who had consistently and visibly spoken out against the coup, calling for the return of democracy and President Aristide, was among them.

One Wednesday afternoon in October 2004, while Fr. Gerry was serving meals at the food program, hooded men working for the interim government's police force circled the St. Clare's rectory. When Fr. Gerry refused to come out, the men stormed the building and demanded that the children lie facedown on the floor. They dragged Fr. Gerry through a window over broken glass and sped off with him in a truck. When they drove away, the police shot into the crowd that had gathered outside the rectory, wounding three children.

Never have I felt so helpless and far away from Haiti as on that day. I received a call just as Fr. Gerry was being taken from the rectory. He had called from his cell phone to alert friends in Miami, who then called me. I sat stunned as I took in the news, my stomach getting tighter and tighter. I had the same all-over heartsick feeling I experienced after Rich died. My hands trembled as I typed out an e-mail to What If? Foundation supporters pleading for them to contact their congressional representatives, the State Department, and Haitian authorities. Other organizations did the same. Thousands of e-mails, faxes, and letters were sent. Fr. Gerry was immediately listed by Amnesty International as a Prisoner of Conscience. Throughout Haiti, Aristide supporters were disappearing— being arrested or killed—so I feared for Fr. Gerry's life every day he was in prison.

Seven weeks later, he was released without charges.

In the tradition of Gandhi and Martin Luther King Jr., he did not stop speaking out against the human rights violations and other injustices against the poor. Fr. Gerry has told me he cannot separate his faith from politics. His example for how to live his life is Jesus. Jesus was not silent about injustice or the oppression of the poor. For Fr. Gerry, speaking out from the pulpit and through the media about the need for change, for the respect of human rights, for the release of political prisoners, for food, water, education, health care, and economic opportunities for all Haitians, not just the wealthy, is a critical part of his ministry.

He was arrested again in July 2005, just a few days after we expanded the food program to four days a week. This time, even though he was again listed as an Amnesty International

Prisoner of Conscience and thousands of letters, faxes, and e-mails were sent on his behalf, he remained in prison for over six months.

It was only after Dr. Paul Farmer of Partners In Health diagnosed Fr. Gerry with leukemia and life-threatening pneumonia that he was given a medical reprieve. He was released from prison on January 29, 2006, to receive treatment in Miami. A few days later, René Préval was democratically elected as Haiti's president. He had served as president from 1996 to 2001 and was the favorite of the poor majority, who had hope that his election would put an end to the violence and repression.

Progress has been slow. Members of the St. Clare's community have told me that it is difficult for Haiti's democracy to fully flourish with UN forces still there, many of the same officials appointed during the coup regime still in place, and most of the political prisoners still behind bars. Although the country is more stable politically, the same deep divisions and power struggles remain.

I visited Fr. Gerry in Miami shortly after his release from prison. Even though he had been through months in a cell, had just had surgery, and was about to go through chemotherapy, he had that same indomitable faith, energy, and hope. And thankfully, after seven months of chemotherapy, the leukemia was, and continues to be, gone.

Although he longs to be back in Haiti full-time, Fr. Gerry is still living in South Florida, regaining his strength. He travels to Port-au-Prince regularly and hopes to return permanently soon. Being physically separated from St. Clare's has not kept Fr. Gerry from being involved in the lives of his parishioners and the community. His passion and vision for the St. Clare's neighborhood and all of Haiti continue to inspire those who know him. He is in daily contact with the leaders of the food and education programs and has helped guide them into strong, self-sufficient operations that are not dependent on his presence. The programs have grown to be integral parts of the community and are run with the integrity, faith, courage, and commitment to serve those in greatest need.

Today, the food program is needed more than ever. A sharp rise in food prices across the globe has sent Haiti into an even deeper hunger crisis. The price of rice worldwide nearly doubled from February through April 2008. As in many countries throughout Asia and the Americas, rice is the primary staple of Haiti. With over half the Haitian population earning less than $1 a day and 78 percent earning less than $2 a day, this increase has made it impossible for most people in Haiti to feed their families. It now costs nearly $1 for one small can of rice. Reports have appeared in the media of families eating "mud cookies"—dirt, mixed with salt and vegetable shortening and baked in the sun—because they don't have the money for food. Food price protests and riots have taken place in several countries around the world, including Haiti. The world is finally taking notice of the suffering, and I pray that this will help bring about positive change.

The main reasons cited for the dramatic global increase in the price of rice, wheat, corn, and other staples are rising fuel costs, a push to create biofuels from cereal crops, weather problems, and an increased demand in China and India. Haiti is especially vulnerable to these price increases because it is dependent on imported food staples.

Haiti is the third-largest importer of rice from the U.S.—240,000 metric tons per year. Until the 1980s, Haiti was self-sufficient in rice production. But in 1986, a multimillion-dollar loan from the International Monetary Fund (IMF) required that tariff protections for Haitian rice and other agricultural products as well as some industries be reduced, opening Haiti's markets up to competition from the outside. Rice from the U.S. began pouring into Haiti. Since it is heavily subsidized by the U.S. government and therefore cheaper than Haitian rice, within a few years most Haitian rice farmers went out of business. Now, with the price of U.S. rice rising and very little domestic rice being produced in Haiti, millions of people throughout Haiti are starving.

In March 2006 we increased the food program to five days a week and have been able to sustain that level ever since. An average of a thousand people are fed each day. Some walk 5 miles from Cité Soleil. Thirty members of St. Clare's Church prepare and serve the meals every Monday through Friday. Children are fed first. A long line of young adults, parents, and the elderly wait near the rectory gate to see if there will be any food left over for them. The cooks try to be sure there always is, but lately, with more children then ever coming to the program, some days there isn't anything left for the adults.

With the dramatic increase in the cost of food, I wonder sometimes whether we'll be able to provide the funding needed to keep it all going. The cost per meal has increased significantly. It has gone from 50 cents to 70 cents per meal and continues to rise. I try to calm myself by remembering the Sunday we ran out of food and how I learned to keep the focus on love—celebrating what we can do, and not lamenting what we can't. I try to focus on the fact that a thousand people a day, five days a week, receive some relief from their hunger, even though millions of Haitians are suffering and providing these meals does not address the root causes of their poverty. I remind myself that visiting doctors have told me they don't see the signs of malnutrition among the majority of children who eat regularly at the rectory, and that Fr. Gerry believes the meals have helped the community remain peaceful during the volatile years since the coup d'état. The food program, he says, remains "an islet in the middle of the ocean . . . A place where people are loved, respected, and fed every week. Hope is kept alive in the midst of troubled days."

Regardless of the obstacles—the coup d'état, the hurricanes, the flood that wiped out a year's worth of construction on St. Jude's Chapel, beatings, prison, leukemia, and the current hunger crisis—Fr. Gerry's belief in the importance and power of small steps remains a guiding force for everyone in the neighborhood and for me, too. Every morning when I sit down at my desk, I look at the sign I have taped to my computer monitor—*"Piti piti na rive,"* Little by little we will arrive—and I feel inspired to continue this work.

My Haitian colleagues continue to be my greatest teachers. Whenever I visit Haiti, Manmi Dèt's open arms welcome me "home." I treasure every minute with her and make sure we sit next to each other at Mass. She'll be 80 years old this year, but she still walks up the hill to St. Clare's when she can, greeting everyone along the way. She and the fifteen ladies in the front left pews continue to pray and sing and hold the space for love, hope, and possibilities with their extraordinary faith.

Manmi Dèt and Nennenn have passed on the responsibilities of the food program to another group of incredible women from St. Clare's. Today, Nennenn is pouring her heart into the construction of a small medical clinic called Clinique St. Michel—a new St. Clare's outreach project funded through the efforts of a physician assistant in Philadelphia—that just opened its doors. Nennenn's daughter, Romi, who recently graduated from medical school in Cuba, is the clinic's doctor. Members of St. Clare's Church have been trained as health agents and are doing health education and advocacy work throughout the Tiplas Kazo community. Manmi Dèt and Nennenn plan to serve meals to the patients at the clinic, so we might be working together again soon.

Over the years, slowly, gradually, organically, one meal at a time, one student at a time, one summer at a time, we've grown. I treasure the intimacy of this work—serving as the link between the women, men, and children who send donations to the What If? Foundation and the members of St. Clare's who run the programs day in and day out. It's a special partnership with a simple structure—direct and effective. This is truly love in action.

One of my greatest personal challenges remains living in balance. I struggle with wanting to do more so we can expand and more children and adults can be served. The need is urgent and the work involved in running the What If? Foundation continues to grow. Yet, part of me craves a slower pace with more time for my family (I've remarried! and Luke is now a teenager), for writing, and for contemplation. I remain the volunteer president and director of the Foundation and still run my health and wellness business part-time, so my days often feel overscheduled and overwhelming. At times, I feel close to burnout, trying to juggle it all. I know I need to find a way to couple the urgency of the situation with the ability to sustain my energy over time—a common challenge for many people.

I often think about the Sunday night when Nennenn led me to the pool in my muumuu and the time she taught me to dance. "Dancing is good for you, Margo," she whispered. Her days included both the commitment to the food program and laughter under the stars. She is able to sweat in the heat of cooking and then shake loose with dancing. She always has time to pray. I've realized that filling every free moment with work, even for a life-and-death cause, is not healthy for me or sustainable, so I now have an assistant in my office. A first step.

I have a picture of Nennenn and Manmi Dèt on my computer screen saver, their arms around each other, smiling, with a twinkle in their eyes. It feels like they're watching over me, encouraging me to find and hold the balance between work and play, action and stillness. When I look at them, I often think of the fruit salad and the love and time they put into it, and I'm gently reminded how I want to live my life.

Fr. Gerry's courage and commitment also remind me of how I want to live. Recently he shared with me an experience he had while in the Haitian National Penitentiary. There was an old man who lived across the street from the prison. Fr. Gerry could see him through the window. The old man was thin and weak. Since St. Clare's parishioners brought food to Fr. Gerry almost every day, he had more than he needed. He and the old man developed a signal. At 6:00 every evening, Fr. Gerry would shine his flashlight at the door of the man's home. One flash meant bring a small pot. Three meant bring a huge pot. The old man came every evening. Fr. Gerry arranged with the guards to let him in so he could receive whatever food Fr. Gerry was able to offer. Nearly every evening while Fr. Gerry was in prison, the old man, his wife, and children from the neighborhood had food to eat.

Time and again, Fr. Gerry and the members of St. Clare's have shown me there is always the opportunity to act and make a difference. There is always hope. Little by little!

Acknowledgments

I wish to thank the many loving, generous people in my life who helped make this story and this book possible, including:

Fr. Gérard Jean-Juste, for his daily example of faith, hope, and love. His courage and commitment to serve those in need, working tirelessly for social justice, are a constant source of inspiration. The privilege of our friendship and partnership is one of the greatest blessings of my life.

Manmi Dèt, Nennen, and all the members of the Dépestre family, for welcoming me "home," taking such good care of Luke, Paul, and me during our visits, and giving their hearts to the food program.

Cloraine Dorissant, Roselie, Wadner Pierre, Jean-Claudel Merisma, Jean-Marie Noel, Porfil, Sonn, Sanon, Michel, Toto, and the dozens of other members of the St. Clare's community in Port-au-Prince, Haiti, who day in and day out have made the food and education programs possible through their courage and dedication.

Barbara Gates, this book's midwife, for her loving kindness and gifts as a writer and editor, which helped me find and trust my voice.

Arnie Kotler at Koa Books, for his belief in this book and giving it flight through his editing expertise, gentle guidance, and collaboration.

My parents, Frederick and Louise Trost, for their unconditional love and lifelong example of putting faith into action. My siblings, Marianne, Christine, Paul, and Sarah, their spouses, Adam, Douglas, Shelly, and John, and children, Grace, Reed, and Simon, for their love and friendship and the great joy we share as a family.

Bryan Sirchio and the Ministry of Money's "Reverse Mission" program, for leading me to Haiti that first, life-changing time.

The Wisconsin Conference of the United Church of Christ for the original gift of $5,000.

The What If? Foundation Board of Directors, for their support and guidance over the years—Carolyn Betz, Bob Ferguson, Bob Fisher, Bonnie Paulson, Bryan Sirchio, Pat Stevens, and Frederick Trost.

The What If? Foundation donors, for their trust in me and support of the Foundation, making it possible to fund the food and education programs at St. Clare's.

Limor Inbar, Grace Maina, Audrey Raya, and Sara Wolf, for providing such wonderful and critical assistance in the What If? Foundation office.

The many people who read the manuscript along the way, offering valuable feedback and encouragement, including Johanna Berrigan, Dr. Walter Brueggemann, Brian Concannon, Ketty Dépestre, Dr. Paul Farmer, Leslie Fleming, Bishop Thomas Gumbleton, Fr. Jean-Juste, Barbara Lagoni, Marilyn Langlois, Jody Parsons, Lorisa Schouela, Kristelle Sim, Thara Srinivasan, Gay Thomas, Loune Viaud, Julie Ann Weiss, and Robin Woodland.

Ayelet Maida, who made the book design so beautiful, Wadner Pierre for his sensitive photos, Mark Rhynsburger for his superb copy editing and proofreading, and publicist Lorna Garano, for her help with spreading the word.

My Shaklee family, for their support every step of the way and patience while I put my business on hold to complete the manuscript.

The many other angels who have come into my life and offered their assistance so generously, including Francine Delica, James and Deby Fellowes, Marjorie Fine, Lavarice Gaudin, Anne Hastings and Fonkoze, Carla Lamothe, Bill Quigley, Steven Rahn, Mirari Romero, Katherine Salazar-Poss, Irene Scully, and Tina Thomson.

My extraordinary son, Luke, wise beyond his years, who brings me such joy and enriches my life every day. I feel so blessed to be his mother.

And finally, my incredible husband, Toma, "my anchor and my kite," whose love and partnership bring immeasurable peace and happiness into my life. It was his idea to write my experience down and his faith in me that helped me believe I could do it.

What If? Foundation

The What If? Foundation is a nonprofit 501(c)(3) charitable organization dedicated to providing hope and opportunity to impoverished children in Haiti.

Programs supported by the What If? Foundation in partnership with members of the St. Clare's community of Port-au-Prince, Haiti include a food program, school scholarships, and a summer camp.

For more information about the What If? Foundation or to make a donation, please visit www.whatiffoundation.org or write to:

What If? Foundation
1563 Solano Avenue, #192
Berkeley, CA 94707

koa books

Koa Books publishes works on personal transformation, social issues, and native cultures.

Please visit www.koabooks.com for a full list of recent and forthcoming titles.

Koa Books
P.O. Box 822
Kihei, Hawai'i 96753
www.koabooks.com